THE RISE AND FALL OF THE POLICE COLLEGE

The Police of New York City

robert l. bryan

Published by robert l. bryan, 2023.

While every precaution has been taken in the preparation of this book, the publisher assumes no responsibility for errors or omissions, or for damages resulting from the use of the information contained herein.

THE RISE AND FALL OF THE POLICE COLLEGE

First edition. July 26, 2023.

Copyright © 2023 robert l. bryan.

ISBN: 979-8223896555

Written by robert l. bryan.

For Meghan

Prologue:

Police Commissioner: Twenty-five years is a long time, Casey. I'm sure you'll enjoy a rest.

Patrolman Casey: A rest?

Police Commissioner: Yes. Casey, I know you're in great shape, but no matter what you think, you're not as good a man as you were twenty-five years ago, or even ten years ago for that matter – none of us are.

Captain: You see, we've got a lot of young men coming out of the Police College, and we have to find room for them.

Police Commissioner: Of course, I don't suppose you'll mind taking that half pay pension check every month for the rest of your life while you take it easy.

The dialogue is from the beginning of *Three Cheers for the Irish*, a 1940 movie about a New York City cop, played by Thomas Mitchell, who is forced into retirement because of his age. It is one of my favorite movies and always a "must see" around Saint Patrick's Day.

As much as I like the movie, something always bothered me. I can't stand when movies and TV shows get technical aspects of the NYPD wrong. The plot and acting may be fantastic, but I will immediately get caught up in that fact that the wrong uniform is being worn, or a sergeant is wearing a police officer's shield. For years, this obsession with realism caused me to wince every time the captain in the above scene muttered the words, "Police College." Who the heck ever heard of a Police College? I attributed it to just another case of Hollywood not doing its homework and getting a technical aspect of the NYPD wrong.

Wasn't I surprised when I learned that there actually was a Police College.

Introduction:

The young police officer let out a slow controlled breath and attempted to loosen his body movements. He tried to convince himself that feeling anxious was normal and natural - a part of the system that evolved to keep him safe and well. It was an alarm system of sorts; one he should heed. He depressed the button on the microphone and acknowledged the "suspicious person" radio call. He squinted as he peered down the long, dimly lit alley. The rattle of a supermarket cart in the distance was audible before the officer could detect any movement. An old cart came into view, rusted and full of tin cans. It shook as it passed over the uneven concrete slabs in the alley. The source of power moving the cart came into focus. It was a shriveled old man with a white beard travelling down his dark overcoat. The officer observed him in silence for a moment. With the homeless it was harder to get a bearing on their age. The officer initiated a friendly greeting, but the man averted his gaze, not meeting the officer's smile. The man kept advancing with his cart and the officer's smile disappeared when he noticed the handle of the knife protruding from his waist as his overcoat flopped open. The officer's voice was loud and firm. "Stop! Put your hands in the air where I can see them!"

The man pushed his cart to the side but did not raise his hands. Instead, he reached to his waist and pulled out the knife, wielding it menacingly toward the officer. The officer pulled the Glock 19 semi-automatic pistol from his holster and assumed a combat shooting stance as he bellowed different commands. "Drop the knife – now!"

The man said nothing as he began his advance toward the officer with his knife at the ready position. He moved slowly at first but picked up speed as he got closer to the officer.

The officer repeated the command in a louder tone. "Drop the knife – now!"

Again, the man paid no attention to the officer's order and kept advancing, raising the knife to a position to perform an overhand thrust.

The officer took a deep breath as he lined up the front and rear sights on his pistol. When the advancing man was approximately six feet from him, he squeezed the trigger twice. The knife flew out of his hand as the man dropped to the concrete. The officer continued covering the man, noting the location of the knife and looking for any movement from the man or from further down the alley. He had to make sure there wasn't a second attacker lurking in the darkness.

"Cut!"

The voice was as loud as the officer's commands to the homeless man, but it didn't belong to another cop on the street or a hiding perpetrator. It was a police academy instructor calling an end to a training exercise.

The officer had not been on patrol in Manhattan when he encountered the man with the knife. In fact, the officer was not wearing the blue uniform of an NYPD police officer. He was wearing the gray uniform of a police academy recruit. The homeless man wasn't really there. He was an image on the screen of a firearms simulation system, a system controlled by an instructor who had the ability to make the homeless man react by complying with the officer's commands, or as in this case, attacking the officer with a knife. The weapon the officer fired was a real Glock 19, but it had been modified for training. The barrel fired a laser instead of a bullet and the recoil the officer felt after firing a shot was caused by a CO_2 cartridge located where the pistol's magazine would normally be. This entire exercise was being conducted in a room in College Point, Queens, inside the New York City Police Academy, the NYPD's state of the art training facility since 2014.

The instructor's critique was not just for the benefit of the recruit who had played out the scenario. It was also for the benefit of the fifteen other recruits nervously waiting for their turns with the simulator.

The recruit's chest swelled with pride when the instructor commented that he had responded to the call of a suspicious male and approached the situation cautiously as he attempted to make contact with the male. He said the recruit's commands were clear and loud as he attempted to get the male to drop the knife.

"Where were you aiming when you fired?" the instructor asked.

"Center mass," the recruit replied.

"Why?"

"Because I was shooting to end the threat by aiming for center mass of the body because it is the largest area of the body."

"Excellent," the instructor praised, "but there were a couple of areas you could have done better."

The recruit's chest delated a bit as the instructor continued. "Once you became aware of the knife you did not seek cover," he said as he pointed to the various props in the room, such as a mailbox and a lamppost. "Also, you could have done a better job attempting to de-escalate."

I know this site in College Point very well. It was my last command in the NYPD before I retired. I was a police academy instructor during my career, but it wasn't at College Point. When I was assigned to the site of the police academy, I was a captain in command of the police auto pound, and this state-of-the-art police training facility was built on the site where I had kept watch over several thousand recovered stolen and evidence vehicles. When I prepared recruit officers for patrol, the academy was in Manhattan, and de-escalation was not an emphasized part of the curriculum.

In today's police academy the recruits have a lot of tools in their toolbox including communication skills, and they must decide which one to use in each simulator scenario. Communication is key, because it plays a huge role when it comes to de-escalating a situation.

NYPD training has changed drastically over the years. Everything at the academy today centers around de-escalation and that's a fairly new innovation. The recruits spend six months going through a total of 913 hours of training: 269 hours focused on academics, 150 hours on physical tactics, 105 hours on firearms and 28 hours on driver training. The additional 361 hours are used for additional add-on trainings and presentations.

When it comes to firearms training, as illustrated in the simulator exercise, the officers "don't shoot to kill." They are taught to shoot to end the threat by aiming for center mass of the body because it is the largest area of the body.

In order to graduate, the recruits must pass the Job Standards Test. It includes, climbing over a 6-foot wall, a stair climb, a physical restraint simulation, a pursuit run, a 180-pound dummy drag, and a trigger pull. Once they graduate, the officers are assigned a field training officer for six months. They remain on probation for two years. Beyond that, officers are brought back in for training at least five days a year. They receive refresher training on their firearms at least twice a year and on their tasers at least once a year.

The academy itself has many different training opportunities. Some of the rooms have been transformed into different scenarios, such as a New York City street, and even apartments with different layouts. In one of the classrooms, recruits respond to a call of an emotionally disturbed man on a subway.

In 2016, the use of force policy was rewritten. For the first time, it included the phrase "duty to intervene". What this means is any officer who witnesses another officer using excessive force must intervene.

This is not the police academy where I was a police science instructor in 1986 and 1987. The police academy in New York City has evolved, and this constant evolution is what continues to make the NYPD one of the best trained police departments in the world.

In the long, proud history of the New York City Police Department training has grown and evolved from next to nothing to the modern technologically advanced training in today's academy.[1]

What makes the NYPD one of the most highly trained police forces in the world is simply the variety of training. Besides recruit training, there is physical training, driver education training, chemical awareness training, tactical training, computer training (digital forensics), civilian training, criminal investigations, and instructor development, which all amounts to their strategy of graduating New York's finest.[2]

The official birth of the NYPD was 1845, and since that time the police academy has had many different names and locations. There was even a period of time when training was conducted at the Police College. That is the subject of this book – the rise and fall of the Police College.

In the Beginning:

The New York City Police Department was not always so highly trained. In fact, there was a time when there was no training at all. Professional, well-trained police are a relatively new phenomenon. During the early history of policing, individual citizens were largely responsible for maintaining law and order among themselves. Those who served as constables and justices of the peace did so voluntarily and were not typically paid for their services and certainly received no formal training.

Shire reeves, or sheriffs, were employed full-time to oversee law enforcement activities within their shires in England and their counties in the colonies. Through the centuries, those practices played a significant role in the history of policing around the world. The loosely based system of social control worked quite well for centuries, particularly in more rural and less populated regions. However, the late 1700s and early 1800s saw a population explosion in major cities in the United States and England. Riots and civil unrest were common, and it became increasingly clear that there was a need for a more permanent and professional form of law enforcement that would carry the official authority of the government.[3]

In the 18th century the village constable was made constable because nobody else in the village wanted to employ him. He was so constituted, both physically and mentally, that his shield of authority was, in effect, a testimonial of the charitable impulse of the villagers. And, in many cities, including New York, there was a time when a policeman was not selected for any particular qualification for the job, but rather because he did not have any other job.[4]

Perhaps the most powerful advocate for a professional, well trained police force was Sir Robert Peel, a Minister of Parliament who served as Home Secretary for the United Kingdom in the 1820s. In 1829, Peel established the Metropolitan Police Services in London. With the founding of London's police force, Peel became widely regarded by criminologists and historians alike as the father of modern policing. British police officers are still known affectionately as "Bobbies" in honor of his first name, Robert.

The concept of a centralized, professional police force was a tough sell initially and was met with a tremendous amount of resistance. The public feared that a police force would essentially behave as another arm of the military. As a result, there was an understandable reluctance to agree to be controlled by what many assumed would be an occupying force. To overcome this opposition, Peel is known for laying the framework for what a police force should be comprised of and how a good police officer should conduct himself. While there is debate as to whether he ever clearly enumerated his ideas in any sort of list format, it is generally agreed that he created what are to this day considered to be the primary principles of policing.

Peel's efforts were very effective in assuaging public fears and concerns. In addition to the principles of policing, Peel and his supporters took other measures to ensure that there was a clear distinction between professional police officers and the military. Police wore blue uniforms in contrast to the bright red of the royal armed forces. They were forbidden to carry guns, and at all times the importance of maintaining the public trust was impressed upon members of the force.

This concept of the modern police force soon found its way to the United States, though it was not implemented in exactly the same manner as it was in London. Due to the extreme political influence during the 19th century, there were virtually no standards for hiring or training police officers. Essentially, politicians within each ward would hire men that would agree to help them stay in office and not consider whether they were the most qualified people for the job. Police officials were appointed through political affiliations and because of this they were frequently unintelligent and untrained.

New policemen heard a brief speech from a high-ranking officer, received a hickory club, a whistle, and a key to the callbox, and were sent out on the street to work with an experienced officer. Not only were the policemen untrained in law, but they operated within a criminal justice system that generally placed little emphasis upon legal procedure. During the period, American police forces were notorious for their corruption and promotion of the "third degree," or torture methods in interrogation. Alexander S. "Clubber" Williams, a corrupt cop in New York's Vice District symbolized the era when he told a reporter that "there is more law in the end of a nightstick than in the decision of the Supreme Court."

The police system as we know it grew out of the old vigilance committees created by the early American communities to protect themselves against public offenders. The voluntary character of these committees and the lack of legal and community control over them led to a whole series of police problems. It was not until 1825 that New York set an example to the rest of the country by organizing the first real police force. But it did duty only during the day; for the night, special watchmen had to be hired who were supposed to guard the city from 9 PM until sunrise. Evidently, their services were not satisfactory, for in 1844 the Legislature authorized the formation of a single day-and-night police force. The first uniformed men appeared on the streets of the city in 1856, and even then, each ward had its own regulations as to the proper clothes to be worn by the policemen.

No efforts had been made by any American police organization to attain anything like standard training until in New York an attempt in this direction was made by Police Commissioner Arthur Wood when a course of instruction for detectives was introduced. The example was followed by other cities. But even then, no social training peculiarly applicable to detective work was offered. This was in contrast with the highly specialized training of members of the detective squads in Europe, especially in Vienna and Paris. In England training for detective work had taken the form of an apprenticeship in plainclothes duty with attention to beggars, pickpockets, bookmakers, and statutory offenders.[5]

The first formal training in New York City came into existence in 1853 with police captains instructing officers in the "School of Soldier" and drill instructors appointed to train and discipline officers in crowd and riot control.[6]

During the latter stages of the 19th century there were very few initiatives in police training. During this era, however, increasing attention was directed to professionalism and training as a result of the public's growing contempt of political corruption and social disorder. For example, in 1877, the Cincinnati Police Department, and in 1903 the Cleveland Police Department established training programs for police recruits where on a weekly basis captains conducted classes that covered state laws, city ordinances and department regulations.

It was not until 1907, however, that August Vollmer, Marshall of the city of Berkeley, California, set forth the idea for the first formal police academy. He was convinced that the principal problems with all police departments was directly related to lack of training, and in 1908 he developed a police school which covered a wide variety of subjects such as police methods and procedures, fingerprinting, first aid, and criminal law.

Following Vollmer's lead, in 1909 the New York City Police Department opened its first police academy which provided recruits with training in firearms, departmental rules and regulations, police procedures and criminal law. But it was Theodore Roosevelt, more than a decade earlier who sowed the seeds for New York City's first police academy.

In 1895 Roosevelt—fearless and righteous and full of zeal—was appointed New York City Police Commissioner and was assigned to clean up the Big Apple at what many said was its dirtiest, most rotten moment in history.

Up until that time the New York City police school usually contained about one hundred recruits with just one instructor. The instructor ran them through military drills and courtesies known as the "school of the soldier" from 10 AM to noon, and then read the rules and regulations in the afternoon. During this period the recruits were taught so little that at the end of their thirty-day training period the majority of them didn't know when an arrest should be made or how to make it. The patrolman of that era didn't ask questions when a stranger came to him and demanded the arrest of another man. The patrolman just went ahead and brought the accused to the station house, with a broken head if necessary, but without any inquiry as to whether a crime had been committed.

In the 1890s, New York City was a bustling chaotic city with no traffic lights and few traffic rules; horse carriages zigzagged any way up and down any street and a small cadre of two dozen tall "Broadway Squad" officers helped pedestrians to cross the major intersections. Four elevated train lines striped the island, spewing coal dust and granting passengers voyeuristic glimpses into second floor windows. Top-hatted swells strutted along Fifth Avenue while immigrants slept in shifts in overcrowded tenements. At night, armies of beggars and streetwalkers accosted anyone and everyone. But beyond all its commerce and prestige, beyond all its Astor high society and its striving immigrants, it was an open secret that New York City was also the vice capital of the United States.

There were 40,000 prostitutes working the streets, charging from 50-cents to $10 a session. And all of it was made possible by the corrupt, look-the-other-way connivance of the police force and of corrupt Tammany Hall politicians.

Police captains shook down brothel madams for big monthly payoffs; corner cops took bribes from bootblacks wanting choice locations and from fruit vendors who wanted to display wares on the sidewalk. The captains of the New York City Police Department in the era before the Mafia were the ones who "organized" crime in their precincts and settled turf disputes. New York City was certainly a wicked place, full of temptations. Tourists and out-of-town businessmen flocked there. That is, until Teddy Roosevelt stepped in.

When Theodore Roosevelt was commissioner, he tried to enforce all the laws and all police conduct rules, to the absolute shock of most New Yorkers. Roosevelt also wanted officers to be courteous to citizens, a concept almost unthinkable at the time. He tried to shut the saloons on Sunday in strict observance of the Sabbath Excise Law, which got him hated by the vast population of beer-drinking, six-day-a-week workingmen. He made special efforts to have fair elections; he helped re-introduce the bigger, more fearsome police night stick, and in September 1895, he and the board pioneered a pistol shooting range. Some police historians credit Roosevelt's practice range as eventually leading to the founding of the first police academy.

In the 1908 school of instruction, recruits were instructed for two hours each day and two more hours in drill and exercises. The recruits were placed on post each night from 8 PM to 12 midnight, with a patrolman to learn the practical mode of discharging their duties.

On their first day, the recruits were given the following notice:

You are hereby informed that as a Probationary Patrolman you are not certain of permanent employment until one month has expired. Incur no expense for uniforms or equipment. Sufficient opportunity will be afforded each man to procure a uniform after the expiration of the probationary period.

The First Academy:

The first New York City Police Academy opened in 1909 at 240 Centre Street in Manhattan. This location was the new police headquarters and for over sixty-four years, police officers called it the big white castle, the nerve center of the nation's largest and most sophisticated police department. Over the years, the New York City Police Department's Centre Street headquarters would combat mobsters, bootleggers, jewel thieves and serial killers. Old Police headquarters, or the Central Office as it was once called, represented one of the most beautiful Beaux-Arts masterpieces Manhattan had to offer. Built between 1905 and 1909 on a wedge-shaped parcel of land bounded by Grand, Centre and Broome Streets where the old Centre Market had stood since 1817, the new headquarters was needed following the consolidation of the five boroughs in 1898, when the police force quadrupled in size.

On midnight November 29, 1909, Police Commissioner William F. Baker inaugurated New York's era of scientific policing when telephone switchboards at the old police headquarters at 300 Mulberry Street were simultaneously shut down and transferred to the new Central Office. On the first floor of 240 Centre Street, visitors would find an ornate reception room. To the left of reception, guests could find the Chief Inspector's office, the Bureau of Information and the Boiler Squad, an NYPD unit responsible for testing steam heaters in buildings throughout the city. Housed on the fourth floor, the City's Police. The facilities included a gym, a drill room, heavy bags and a running track. The cellar boasted a pistol shooting range, the property clerk, and 72 cells for high profile Detective Bureau prisoners.

The cellar also contained a deep, dark secret. According to popular lore, a tunnel was bored to connect Callahan's (now called ONieals) with Police HQ, thereby creating easy passage for the Boys in Blue to enjoy a drink during the trying days of Prohibition. ONieals (the official spelling deprives it of two apostrophes) was established as Callahan's around 1880. The tunnel, while providing undetected access for cop drinking, is now part of the wine cellar. An upstairs brothel held court at one point, and the joint was run as a speakeasy during the dry years. The NYPD headquarters was eventually retired in 1973, leaving the property in vacancy for the next decade. The tunnel is still visible in ONieals and is used today as the wine cellar. In 1987, the headquarters was sold, turned into luxury residential condos and the tunnel was filled. These luxury condos, commissioned as a NYC landmark, housed some well-known names including Steffi Graf, Winona Ryder and Christi Turlington.

The Police Department officially closed 240 Centre Street in 1973, moving headquarters to One Police Plaza. In a testament to the stupidity of the city bureaucracy, rather than relocating the historic records into an archive, the department unceremoniously dumped a half-century worth of police records into the East River.

Roosevelt's emphasis on police professionalism and training had its growing pains. Just as Londoners in Peel's time had concerns about a professional police force turning into an army of occupation, Roosevelt's new and improved professionally trained New York City Police Department evoked the same fears. The problem was that militarization and training are synonymous. Effective militaries are always well trained. In the years leading up to, during, and following the United States' 1917 entrance into World War I, the NYPD's transition from the hulking 19th century bruisers of Gangs of New York to modern police officers was cemented by how preparedness and militarization effected the way NYPD officers acted, looked, and understood their jobs.

From 1915 through 1917, "preparedness" became a central tenet of Police Commissioner Arthur Woods' department, whether it be for fire, flood, cyclone, tidal wave, earthquake, or even foreign invasion.

Of course, preparing a police force for a foreign invasion also meant remaking it as a military force to be reckoned with.

Many New Yorkers looked on with anxiety as preparedness transformed the NYPD into what resembled a militarized occupation of the city. In one training exercise, police were sent to Staten Island in companies of 350 men, given military rifles and tactics training, and forced to defend a fort during a "sham battle." On October 17, 1916, the NYPD paraded down Fifth Avenue in a fashion they had never done before. Gone were the signature blue uniforms, or the batons hanging from their belt. Now, New Yorkers saw their neighborhood police officers clad in khaki military-style uniforms with rifles on their shoulders and mounted machine guns being pulled on tripods.

As men and as consumers, police were forced to perform preparedness in ways that effected both their wallets and their waistlines. It was during the years leading up to the U.S. entrance into World War I that gymnasiums were built in stationhouses around the city and department administrators obsessively attempted to manage the physique of their officers. Requiring police to cultivate slimmer more disciplined bodies served the dual function of demonstrating a more soldierly appearance while simultaneously promoting food rationing as healthy and eventually, patriotic. In the first days of January 1917 NYPD designated recruits were made part of the experimental Diet Squad. These husky police officers in training were mandated to live off 25-cents a day. In their daily newspapers, New Yorkers read about the public weigh-ins, meals, and exercise regimens of the men of the Diet Squad. Although the men ultimately gained rather than lost weight, the public attention heaped on the squad's members still succeeded in promoting one message: rationing food doesn't mean starving or even sacrificing.

It was also during this period of time that the importance of the firearms training instituted by Theodore Roosevelt two decades earlier was emphasized. The 1914-1917 Police Department Annual contained the following section:

THE POLICEMAN AND HIS REVOLVER - A policeman's revolver is his most important weapon. It is his last reliance. When the critical time comes that he must fire, therefore, especially in defense of his own life, or the life of another, he must be able to fire straight and true. Failure to hit the mark may mean the life of some innocent person. At best a revolver is a dangerous weapon. It is doubly dangerous when used by the incompetent or careless. A policeman should keep his gun clean and in serviceable condition; his ammunition should be of good quality, and he should carry extra cartridges for one complete reloading. Occasional aiming and firing exercises, even without cartridges, will help. The practice will be more fruitful with cartridges, providing the man is consistent, painstaking and zealous to discover his errors and faults and to correct them.

In times past, policemen received no instruction whatever in the use or care of firearms. Until Roosevelt's emphasis on marksmanship, the entire rank and file of the department lacked any real knowledge or training in this important part of their duty. It was left to the individual to train himself or not, according to his inclination, and as the importance of the efficient use of firearms had never been impressed on the men, the result was, as a matter of course, lack of skill and of interest. The marksmanship of the force was thoroughly bad, and the innocent bystander was in grave danger. It wasn't until Theodore Roosevelt was Police Commissioner from 1895 to 1897 that the revolver became a standard piece of police equipment and firearms training became mandated. Beginning with inspectors and captains, every member of the force received a thorough course of instruction in the care, handling and use of firearms, including safety first principles, mechanism, ammunition, loading and unloading, cleaning, aiming and firing.

In 1917 the Police Training School taught recruits Jiu Jitsu so that they would not have to use their clubs. They were taught to shoot straight so if they had to shoot, they would shoot an escaping felon and not an innocent bystander. Recruits were taught to scale a ladder so that they could be of help in rescuing people from fires. Because patrolmen were on their feet eight hours at a stretch, they were given exercises which developed the muscles of the foot and made it possible for them to work with comfort instead of suffering from what was known as flat feet or broken arches. Recruits were taught how to ride a horse and a motorcycle, and they were taught to swim. In the classroom, the recruits were taught the law which they needed in the every-day life of a policeman, and they were instructed in the methods of careful observation.

It is also important to note that it was during this era that the first real screening of police officer candidates was initiated. In June 1914, a squad of lieutenants was organized for the purpose of investigating the character of civil service candidates applying for appointment to the police department. During the first three and a half years of this squad's existence, about 15 per cent of the men on the eligible list for patrolman were rejected because of previous records, criminal and otherwise.

It was also during this era that the police training school was utilized for more than recruit training. The first development was with reference to the training of higher-ranking officers. Formerly officers were promoted without having had any training or instruction in the duties of the higher rank, each man being forced to get along as well as he could and pick up for himself as best he might, knowledge of his new duties and responsibilities. This was unfair, both to the individual and the department, and both suffered. The department started classes in the training school for patrolmen about to be promoted to sergeant, for sergeants about to be promoted to lieutenant; and men were not made captains or inspectors until they had first been tried out in the higher rank. In order to improve still further the work of the higher ranks, all lieutenants and sergeants were brought to the training school in small classes to be instructed, in drill, handling of men, and leadership.

The training school gave great attention to the physical side of the work. Every man had to keep in as good physical condition as possible, and thorough and vigorous training was given to recruits in drill, drilling with rifles, calisthenics, wrestling and boxing.

Early in 1916 some policeman suggested that it would be a very helpful thing if arrangements could be made so that members of the force could have the chance to study criminal law. The matter was looked into but could not be put into effect due to the great pressure on police work due to World War I. In 1917, however, the matter was again taken up and the course was finally arranged. The subjects were: Criminal Law, Criminal Procedure, Municipal Government, Criminology and Evidence. The hours were so arranged as to afford an opportunity to patrolmen performing night duty to attend the day courses, and those performing day duty to attend the night courses. The fee was $11. Four hundred and fifty-eight members of the department applied for admittance, but war came upon the country at this time, and the original plans could not be carried out. In spite of the extra calls for police service, however, 157 policemen registered and succeeded in completing the course. These men gave up their own time and paid their own money, for the sake of making themselves better policemen.[7]

The Road to College:

The reforms to police training and the eventual establishment of the Police College were mostly due to the work of two police commissioners. Richard Enright was Police Commissioner from 1918 until 1925. He was the first man to rise from the rank-and-file to assume command of the NYPD and, until the appointment of Lewis Joseph Valentine, he was the longest serving commissioner.

Enright joined the NYPD in 1896 and slowly rose through the ranks to police lieutenant and, although a public unknown, he was highly popular on the force as a champion for the rank-and-file officers while president of the Police Lieutenants' Benevolent Association. His popularity and pro-union views had a negative impact on his career however, most especially his criticism of the policies of Mayor John Purroy Mitchel's administration, resulting in his being passed over for promotion to police captain three times "for the good of the service."

A change in administrations enabled Enright to succeed Frederick H. Bugher as Police Commissioner, becoming the first police officer to be appointed from within the ranks. Bugher had incurred the wrath of Mayor John Hylan for his resisting the mayor in his attempts to interfere with the police department by refusing to take "guidance." Enright proved to be more open to Mayor Hylan and was officially appointed commissioner on January 23, 1918. As time went on however, even Enright would reach his limits as the mayor continued in his efforts to control the police force. As a result of Hylan's meddling, Enright became the scapegoat for the mayor's controversial decisions.

Enright was also able to institute a number of reforms and was greatly able to improve working conditions for police officers while in office. He allowed a day off for officers after every six days on duty, oversaw the buildup of large police relief funds and improved the pension system. He also reduced the number of precincts for better management, set up a special police unit to handle vice and gambling on a city-wide basis, reorganized the arrest-quota based merit system and established the first NYPD police camp where ill or wounded officers could recover until they were able to return to duty. One of the most important reforms Enright accomplished was a major change to training in the department.

In 1909 with the new police headquarters on Centre Street came a new police training school on the fourth floor of the building. The training school served its purpose well for the time, but Enright had a vision of something far more expansive. He wanted a state-of-the-art police academy that would be the hub for all department training, not just the training of police recruits.

On February 27, 1925, 150 rookies were graduated from the police training school. The graduation was held at the 69th Regiment Armory at 26th Street and Lexington Avenue and was attended by Police Commissioner Enright and Military Captain Charles E. Schofield, commander of the school. An exhibition of the physical training received during the three months of training was conducted and a dance followed the ceremony. It would be the last graduation from the current police training school.[8]

Commissioner Enright's new Police Academy opened its door on April 24, 1925, marking the end of the old training school. In General Order 15 Commissioner Enright announced eight classes of instruction to be conducted at the new police academy. Deputy Inspector John J. Noonan was appointed commanding officer. The new academy would take over the building that was formerly the Commerce Department of the College of the City of New York on Lexington Avenue and 23rd Street.

Enright's announcement:

In pursuance of the general policy of the present police administration, the Training School, the Detective Training School, and the School of Equitation have been consolidated into the Police Academy, which is to be inaugurated in the Commerce Building of the College of the City of New York on the 24th day of April.

Each of these schools, now consolidated, will be enlarged in scope and supplemented in such a manner as to produce graduates who will be more competent to fulfill the respective duties of the various branches of the force for which they are destined.

The training of members of the force has heretofore been extremely promiscuous and without a definite policy, a method which has not only entailed a loss of time but has failed to secure as high a quality of efficiency in the training and conduct of the force of the Police Department as would have been desirable.

To forestall the further continuation of such conditions it has been determined to establish an academic police training school which would identify individual talent for various forms of police work, train it, and locate it where such talent would be put to the best advantage.

The original departments of instruction were as follows:
- Department of recruits
- Department of Special Services
- The Policewomen
- The Police Clerk
- Motor Transportation
- The Department of Traffic and Safety
- The Department of Horsemanship
- The Department of Detectives
- The Department of Criminal Identification
- The Department of Officer Training
- The Department of Instructor Training

Enright said the new academy would be an improved Scotland Yard and would be the standard for police training around the world. The instructors would be from both within and outside the department with the outside instructors bringing expertise in specialties beneficial to police officers.[9]

The formal opening ceremonies were officiated by Commissioner Enright. Mons. Charles A. Cassidy of Brooklyn delivered the invocation and the Police Glee Club supplied entertainment before Enright officially opened the academy by stating it was destined to become the greatest police training facility in the world.[10]

Newly appointed Deputy Inspector Noonan took command of the Police Academy while Military Captain Charles Schofield, the former commander of the old police training school, provided a surprise when he filed for retirement.

Enright's decision to put Noonan in charge of the new police academy was actually made two years earlier. Noonan was secretly sent to Europe to make a tour and inspection of the great police schools in England, Italy, France, Germany, and Austria. He spent a long period of time at each school, the result being that he brought to the new police academy a full knowledge of what had been accomplished in the older schools of Europe.

John Noonan was born in Ireland and came to the United States at the age of sixteen. He quickly showed his devotion to his new country by joining the old 69th Regiment. He joined the police department in 1903 and for many years was Captain Schofield's subordinate, which may explain Schofield's sudden retirement.[11]

Captain Schofield, who was a drill master in the United States Army was made sergeant in 1906 and lieutenant in 1911. Enright approved a legislative bill authorizing the police commissioner to appoint a military captain of the police department in 1918 and appointed Schofield to the position. Schofield had been in charge of police training for 18-years.[12]

Inspector Noonan's rise in the department was rapid, especially since Commissioner Enright came into office in 1918. He was a patrolman from 1903 until 1913, when he was made sergeant. He went to the officer's training school in Plattsburg after the declaration of war on Germany, came out as a lieutenant and was assigned to duty on the

Provost Guard in charge of the New York City district. He was made lieutenant of police, a captain in 1924 while in Europe, and Deputy Inspector in January of 1925.

Noonan was a big proponent for change in the department. He characterized the typical policeman in the 1890s as a portly, pugnacious man with a big moustache or a full beard, who drank regularly on the job and after a few years became fat. He continued that brute force, more than intelligence, was at a premium in those days and the night stick was used freely. Noonan explained that a new era in policing had to offer a substitute for the flying "billy," and that substitute was training.

Inspector Noonan further commented that in the 1890s men from the building trades formed the great part of the police force, but that at the present time men got too much money laying bricks to consider police work. He continued to say that the "white collar" man was becoming attracted to the force not only by its spirit of adventure but because of the economics of the case – 25-years enlistment at fair pay and then retirement at half pay.

Inspector Noonan then tried to dispel the myth that white collar men would not make good cops by claiming they made equal, if not better cops than the rest. The reason was because police work had become much more intricate and required more brain work. Noonan pointed out that the rookie was expected to learn 42 classifications of crimes; eleven kinds of evidence; all the important branches of the borough, municipal, state, and national governments, and the dozen and a half courts in the city. Such knowledge was not expected in the 1890s.[12]

The work of the new academy began immediately with 250 recruits, 100 detectives, and 15 policemen in the school of equestrianism.[13]

The new academy was only one of the steps taken to raise the standards of the New York force. It was planned to build up a more highly professional organization by three methods:

• Stricter selection of recruits

• More thorough training

• Special training that would be given to candidates for promotion who had passed civil service examinations for new ranks (promotional training).[14]

Some in the newspaper media poked fun at the new academy and the attempt to raise the standards of training within the police department. One 1925 editorial was ahead of its time in referring to the new academy as a police college.

The New York City Police Department has come to a conclusion that knowledge is power and acting on that premise they are opening a police college. Don't be surprised if you see a lot of flat-footed blokes marching around with arms entwined singing "Schooldays."

A woman rushed up to a passing cop the other day and said, "Officer, there's a burglar in my home."

"I'm sorry, madam," answered the cop, "but I have a condition in French, and I am not able to arrest anybody until I work it off."

The entrance examinations will be very stiff. "They shall not pass" seems to be the examiner's motto.

These examinations will consist of such tests as "Button, button, who's got the button," and "Hide and seek."

A rookie cop who had just taken the physical tests met a friend:

"How do you feel?" asked the friend.

"I'm a little stiff," answered the cop.

"I know that, but how do you feel?" said the friend.

There is going to be no freshman class at the Police College, as most of the applicants are already that way.

There is going to be a special course in accountancy to enable the cops to account for their absence when the inspector reports them off post.

The fruit stand peddlers are against the idea of a police college. The cops only swipe apples and bananas now, but the peddlers are afraid that they will be educated up to grapefruit.[15]

For those who may not be familiar, "stiff" is a somewhat outdated slang term for drunk, but it was regularly used in the 1920s. The author of the editorial was taking a swipe at the prevalence of drinking on the NYPD at the time by indicating that the applicant for police college as well as the entire freshman class was "stiff."

At the first graduating class of the new police academy Enright said, "This is the finest representation possible to show the taxpayers of New York City just what they are getting for their money in the way of police protection." He was addressing over two thousand spectators at the 69th Regiment Armory on Lexington Avenue. The class consisted of 275 graduating recruits. The program consisted of exhibitions in calisthenics, jiu-jitsu, boxing, first aid, infantry drill, and a parade review. Attendees included police representatives from Italy, Honduras, Chile, Brazil, Mexico, Norway, Columbia, and Panama.[16]

On June 17, 1925, the routine of the Police Academy was broken by Inspector Noonan's order to have the largest classroom filled with as many students and staff members as possible at 10 AM.

No one knew the reason for the assembly, and it was still a mystery when Noonan entered the room ahead of a large gentleman who no one recognized. The mystery was solved when the Inspector announced that Commissioner Enright had appointed William "Big Bill" Edwards as Special Deputy Commissioner in charge of the Police Academy.

The 300-pound former college football player addressed the assembled audience. "I'm glad to be back in school again, although I have never really left the hall of learning. Inspector Noonan will still run the day-to-day operations of the academy as I will be more of a chum to you than a master. I am not stuck on high-brow stuff and never was. I came from a farm like your own commissioner, and I believe more in the exercise of plain common sense than some of this loftier material. Common sense is the most valuable asset of a policeman as well as that of anyone else. You ought to be proud to be connected with the force that consists of thousands of men who are giving their guts for the benefit of their city. The policemen of New York are the heroes of the city's life. You are to carry on the tradition of the force, as this old college building is carrying on its traditions as an educational center. The police force of New York City was never as efficient as it is today, and it is your privilege and duty to carry on. I'm here to help you, and while I will not be one of your instructors and teach you fellows, I'll be your friend."

There was prolonged applause for the new academy boss, and then Inspector Noonan spoke, assuring the Deputy Commissioner that the men would stand by him.[17]

William Edwards was born in Lisle, New York in 1874. He entered St. John's Military Academy in 1892, graduating in 1896. He entered Princeton University and graduated with a B.S in 1900. He was a prominent figure in the athletic life of the university, and after receiving his degree he remained for a year as coach of the football team and was for several years a member of the football advisory committee. As a member of the football team, and later as its captain, his ability and his power to inspire men made him famous. The greatest moment of his leadership came with the great game against Yale in the fall of 1899 when with Princeton trailing 10 to 8, he called his men around him, inspired them with new courage, ordered an unusual play, and ended up winning the game with 38-seconds to go.

Upon graduation Edwards went to work for an insurance firm in Manhattan. In 1907 he was appointed Deputy Street Cleaning Commissioner by Mayor McClellan, and in 1909 he became the Street Cleaning Commissioner, and was reappointed to the position by Mayor Gaynor.

While with Mayor Gaynor in 1910 on the deck of the Kaiser Wilhelm der grosse, Mayor Gaynor was shot. "Big Bill" Edwards jumped on the mayor's assailant and threw him to the ground after the shooter fired two additional shots at Edwards one of which inflicted a flesh wound to Edwards' arm. For his actions he was awarded a Carnegie Hero Medal. In 1915 he was nominated as an independent candidate for sheriff, but withdrew in favor of Al Smith, who became governor. Edwards was appointed Collector of Internal Revenue in 1917 by President Wilson and served until 1921.[18]

Not everyone was impressed with the appointment of Big Bill. The Standard Union newspaper pointed to Commissioner Enright's remarks in appointing Edwards and commented that if not for Enright's normal somber nature they would have considered his words a joke.

"Bill, you know, was in charge of athletics at Princeton University and he is a big, all-around man. He is a good clean up man, having been born in Broome County and having been head of the Street Cleaning Department."[19]

Big Bill's first innovation in police training was introducing football rules and ethics into the training curriculum, as he hoped to show the New York policemen the value of team play.

In the athletic world of America "Big Bill" Edwards had been known since his days on the Princeton Football team in 1897. For two successive years the giant player – six feet tall and weighing 261 pounds – was right guard, while during his third and senior years he was team captain. Those were banner days for Princeton, and Captain Bill carried the team to a championship.

The new Deputy Commissioner's first great thrill received from football came at the age of 15, in New York City. While crossing Madison Square, Bill saw the Yale team leaving the old Fifth Avenue Hotel for the Polo Grounds, where they were scheduled to play

Princeton. The impression of the players never left him, and he went on to become one of Princeton's greatest football stars.

After graduating in 1900 he coached at both Princeton and Annapolis, and until 1907 umpired at many of the big intercollegiate games. Bill Edwards saw many similarities between the police department and a football team, and he believed the police academy offered the police recruit a chance to put the ball between the posts.

Edwards characterized the similarities this way. "A policeman, like a football player, must make his downs before he can reach the goal. The police academy will offer the opportunity to the student entering it to attain whatever goal he sets for himself. Two elements are necessary to gain a victory: brain and brawn. On the gridiron, as on the patrolman's beat, the latter, without the former is useless. The same is true if you reverse the order. Mind and muscle must complement each other. Both the athlete and the policeman are picked men. They must have physical strength and quickness of mind. They must always be alert and ready for action. In both fields a man can only succeed by giving his best. To do that he must be equipped with gray matter. And again, both games must be played on the level. They are old institutions, and in both the fundamental principles are the same: honesty, courage, physical and mental strength."

The Deputy Commissioner also liked to tell the story of Dennis O'Neil in making his comparison between football and policework. "O'Neil was working for the Yale team. Now, Dennis was a handsome fellow, big and husky. When the trainers looked him over, they thought he had the makings of a good player. But Denny had one weakness. He couldn't learn the signals. Without signals, football is a farce. Denny would always start off in the wrong direction. At last, he got his final warning. Either he must learn or go. He studied all night. The next day he came out onto the field and got in line for practice. But again, he ran amuck. Disgusted, he threw his mask to the ground and exclaimed, 'To hell with your mystic signs and symbols! Show me my man!' There have been many in the force who, figuratively speaking, shared Denny's opinion that muscle and the opponent's countenance were all that are required for the winning of the game. In much the same manner, the old-fashioned policeman believed it his duty to arrest indiscriminately, without exercising discretion. Today, the cop uses discretion, and men aren't needlessly dragged to the stations. He knows when not 'to hit.' The officer is becoming more highly skilled in his profession, and it is to further his efficiency that the academy with its courses of study and its high ideals and aims has been established."

When his football comparisons were completed, Big Bill Edwards was less specific about his actual plans for developing the police academy. "I haven't outlined anything definite as yet. I'm just creeping. Of a few things I am certain, though. I shall inaugurate no highbrow systems, nor do I mean in any way to break down old traditions that have met with the Commissioner's approval. No changes are going to be made without his O.K."[20]

An innovation at the new police academy was having experts from outside the department conduct some of the classes. Commissioner Enright, as commander of the largest fleet of motor vehicles in use in any city in the world with 700 cars, decided to apply the Ford efficiency methods to the cars in use by the department, most of them being Fords. To that end, he initiated in the academy a School of Motor Transportation in which experts from Ford would create forty expert police officers to be spread among the precincts in the city. Edsel Ford was present at the academy to see the beginning of the new program.[21]

In some instances, the expert instructors were celebrities. Legendary magician and escape artist Harry Houdini joined the police academy staff to lecture both recruits and experienced detectives on spiritualistic fakers and other fraudulent sleight of hand performers. Houdini had a long connection with the police department since he mystified famous detective Tommy Byrnes with the ease in which he escaped from Byrnes' handcuffs and leg shackles. Since that time Houdini had performed many exhibitions for the police, but this was the first time he was providing formal instruction in a classroom setting. During one class, the subject focused on the tricks mediums employed to work upon the credulity of wealthy, grieving people. He explained at the outset of the class that he still had an unclaimed standing offer to pay $1,000 to any medium who could honestly produce spirit writing. With the aid of a detective in the class Houdini performed some of the spirit writing tricks he had used so often in his exhibitions. He then performed a variety of tricks used by phony mediums, such as making spirit hands appear and ringing bells in the dark. He told the students that he would reveal how these tricks were performed in later classes and emphasized that it was necessary for the officers to know these tricks in order to expose the actions of the thieving charlatans.[22]

Houdini even held a field trip for his students. The trip was to the home of 30-year-old Mrs. Cecil A. Cook, a medium residing at 41 West 88th Street. Mrs. Cook had advertised a séance in the basement of the home and Houdini and a group of his police students attended. They didn't attend as a famous magician and a group of policemen. Houdini disguised himself as a decrepit old man, and was accompanied by Police Inspector David McAuliffe, Policewoman Elizabeth Michaels, Patrolmen Green and Ryan from the Special Service Squad, and about 25 other police recruits and newspapers reporters, all disguised as believers who paid to attend a real séance.

Mrs. Cook, believing her audience to be sincere seekers of messages from the spirit world, turned down the lights and announced she was a "trumpet medium" and was able to converse with departed souls through a power given to her by God. Beside her on a table in a pan of water were two trumpets, through which, she said, the spirit messages would be transmitted.

The spirit trumpet is a cylindrical cone with a narrow mouthpiece that usually expands in three parts into a megaphone similar to the traditional speaking trumpets employed by cheerleaders at sporting events.

Houdini, in order to make the "spirit voices" speak up, pretended to be hearing impaired. He asked Mrs. Cook to connect him with his fictitious deceased son and instructed her to ask his son to speak loudly. After the customary preliminaries the voice of the "son" came through the trumpet.

"Hello, dad," said the son in a childish treble.

"Hello, Alfred," said Houdini. "How are you?"

Something was apparently interfering with the son's conversation. Mrs. Cook, in the center of the circle, turned to Policewoman Michaels, who previously had complained of a physical ailment. "Your brother Frank is calling you," Cook said. "No," she corrected, "it is your father."

Policewoman Michaels explained later that she had no brother Frank and that her father was very much alive. "Ask Frank if I should go west for my health," said the policewoman.

"No," promptly replied the voice of brother Frank. "You need not make the journey if you will drink plenty of milk and stay out in the fresh air."

At this point Houdini suddenly turned his flashlight on Mrs. Cook in time to catch her removing a tiny metal trumpet from her lips. She collapsed. Policewoman Michaels turned on the lights. Several visitors who did not know a police class / raid was being conducted received back the $1 price of admission. Mrs. Cook and her assistant were transported to the West 68th Street station house to be held until arraignment in West Side Court.[23]

Not everyone was convinced that a celebrity instructor like Houdini was beneficial to police training. An editorial in the Brooklyn Daily Eagle expressed the folly of such training:

In the average mind the reflection persists that a uniformed policeman might pound the New York pavements for his natural life and never catch an Ectoplasm picking a pocket, or slugging a bank messenger, or murdering a jeweler in his store, or setting fire to the Equitable Building. Houdini didn't tell these enthusiastic young sleuths anything worthwhile in practical efficiency. What they need to know is how to tackle not an ectoplasm, but a murder mystery.[24]

The editorialist most likely preferred the curriculum of another celebrity instructor. Benny Leonard was a professional boxer who held the lightweight championship for eight years from 1917 to 1925. He is widely considered one of the all-time greats and was ranked 8th in Ring Magazine's list of the "80 best fighters in the last 80 years." Leonard was made an honorary consulting physical instructor at the Police Academy. In the academy gym he gave a series of boxing demonstrations to 100 recruits. Leonard boxed one round each with two of the recruits showing each how to get a blow in without their adversary being able to return it.[25]

Nine days after assuming the office of Special Deputy Commissioner, Big Bill Edwards held a press conference to provide his vision for the police academy in a very lengthy speech that was part state of the union and part recruitment drive.

"When all our plans are carried out fully the New York Police Academy will take a leading position among the specialty schools of the world. When Police Commissioner Enright combined the three old schools of the police department into the new academy, he had a vision of a day when the police department should be recruited from men of high talents, well trained in all the departments of their work and equally as well fitted for the profession of policeman as is the graduate of the technical school for his profession.

It will be our task to realize that vision, and I expect that before I get through with my share of it I shall have to call on all the fighting qualities I cultivated on the football field in battling for Princeton; shall have to utilize all the mental equipment that nature and my various schools have endowed me with; shall have to study again as I did in the days when I wore the orange and black; shall have to employ what ability in leadership I may have acquired as Street Cleaning Commissioner and as a football coach, and shall have to be again a bit of a diplomat that I found it necessary to be when I was collector of internal revenue.

This is a big fight we have on our hands in the carrying on to higher plane the fight Commissioner Enright has been making for fifteen years to raise the quality and standard of the police force. He has succeeded in leading his men into a position of higher public esteem by a process of raising their whole morale and perfecting their training. He has ever had in view a vision of a police force composed of men who have chosen the profession because of its wonderful combination of public service with the spice of adventure. The Commissioner expressed at the recent International Police Conference a hope for a day when the police forces shall be perfected along the lines at which he aims, when there shall no longer be need of standing armies, and the security of the peoples of the earth will rest on the trained men of the police.

The creation of the police academy is the first step toward his realization of these ideas. When we have succeeded in making it what he hopes for, it will be so famous as a school that it will attract students. Animated by the desire to serve the public they will be drawn to the New York school because it will offer the finest curriculum if its kind in the world.

Something of this fact is already being felt through the hundreds of applications from cities outside of New York for copies of the syllabus of the school and for literature concerning its operation. The chiefs of police of many cities have been stirred to emulating the work of the academy.

How greatly the advancement of the academy to a high position is apt to increase the number of men coming into the police department and improve their average quality may be judged from the experiences

Commissioner Enright has had through giving encouragement to athletes last year.

With just three small athletic teams organized in 1924 the Commissioner found the department was at once attracting a new class of recruits, namely athletes from college football and baseball teams and star performers of the track. The athletic activities in several cases determined the choice the men made of police work as a profession. We expect the same result on the mental side when the police academy offers a real professional training.

While the academy is to do many other things and will have important work in assisting the department in picking out specialists for the various branches of its activities, it will also become a great force for the betterment of the New York police.

In passing it may be said that police work is becoming more and more the work of specialists, the men in different divisions being required to improve themselves as experts in certain lines of work. This tendency has now been going on for several years. With the advent of the motor and the radio and the introduction into the department for special training of detectives has made itself especially manifest in the last year or so.

For the purposes of the specialized department the police academy with its various kinds of training is the ideal institution, yet that side of the work is but our secondary task. Our primary effort must be in the direction of first bringing into the department the highest class of recruits possible – men who want to take up police work as an honorable profession – men who while they have the brawn they must have for this work, will couple these exercises with that of brain.

So, I want to appeal to the red-blooded young men of New York and especially to those who are just now leaving school to start upon their life careers, to enlist in the highly honorable work of guarding the safety of their fellow men. The profession of the police is a rising one: they will find themselves favorites of the public; they will have an opportunity to rise as

Commissioner Enright rose to the second highest position in the greatest municipality in the world.

This is a great opportunity that the police offer, an opportunity that should appeal to men of many classes. In the position of policeman, a man can satisfy that elementary craving for power that is inherent in all of us, can exercise his love for his fellow man by his guardianship of them, and can satisfy the appetite for an open-air activity and for adventure that is the birthright of every he-man.

The appeal is there. I hope that the enrollment in the team will be great, and I am sure I shall enjoy my task as the head coach for the greatest team in the world – the 13,000 men of the New York Police Department."[26]

I especially liked the part about the police department fulfilling the craving for power found in every he-man.

Oh, by the way, forty-four days later, William "Big Bill" Edwards, the self-proclaimed head coach of the greatest team in the world, resigned from the police department to take a position as president of the new American Football league, a professional league created to compete with the National Football League. The American Football League folded after one season.[27]

The departure of Big Bill Edwards did not stop Commissioner Enright from instituting innovative training programs at the Police Academy. Enright sent out a general order that required every member of the department to become a good swimmer, expert in the art of saving a potential drowning victim. On a hot August morning Commissioner Enright was present at Orient Point in Sheepshead Bay to watch 235 non-expert swimmers who were recruits in the academy class, receive swimming instruction from Captain Charles Scully, chief swimming instructor for the American Red Cross. Scully volunteered his services at the suggestion of Inspector Noonan.[28]

Police Commissioners have pet projects that may not be so important to an incoming commissioner. When Richard Enright took office, he quickly discontinued one of the favorites of his predecessor, Arthur Woods, the monthly police bulletin. When talk within the department would drift to what would be affected in a post-Enright police department, the police academy was usually identified as a potential casualty. Commissioner Enright's new police academy had been a thorn in the side of many members of the detective force. In September of 1925 eight detectives were sent back to uniform duty, including the son of a former alderman who had been a detective for a generation. The reasons given for the transfers was that the men had flunked examinations and did not obtain a passing score in the detective training school. Many members of the department, especially detectives, drooled at the prospect of a department without the current police academy.[29]

In November 1925 Jimmy Walker won the mayoral election signaling the end of the road for Commissioner Enright, who was too closely associated with Mayor Hylan for Walker to even consider keeping him in place. Although his eight-year tenure as commissioner received heavy criticism at the time of his resignation, mostly as the result of controversial actions of then Mayor John F. Hylan, his accomplishments and successes were eventually recognized as valued contributions during his near 30-year service on the police force.

On December 27th Commissioner Enright graduated his last class from the police academy and made a surprise promotion by appointing Sergeant Arthur Wallender, physical director of the academy, as military captain.[30]

Mayor Walker had the distinction of appointing four police commissioners during his time in office. His first two commissioners served for relatively short periods of time.

George Mclaughlin was his first appointment. McLaughlin was born in Brooklyn in 1887. He was the son of a ferry boat captain. After graduating high school, he went to work for the North Side Bank in Brooklyn and took night courses at the New York University

School of Commerce. He received a bachelor's degree and went on to become a certified public accountant. Mclaughlin had a friendly relationship with Governor Al Smith, and he served as New York State Superintendent of Banks from 1920 to 1926. It was Governor Smith who was credited with influencing incoming New York City Mayor Jimmy Walker to name Mclaughlin as Police Commissioner on January 1, 1926. Through extensive reorganization McLaughlin improved the department's efficiency and by the end of the year he reported a 44 percent decrease in robberies. In July 1926, however, he organized a special squad to stamp out gambling. Raids were made on political clubhouses of Tammany leaders, among others and political pressure was put on Mayor Walker. The mayor and his police commissioner began to disagree on most issues involving the police department. Finally, Mclaughlin resigned in March of 1927.[31]

Attorney Joseph A. Warren, a life-long friend and former law partner of Mayor Walker was named Police Commissioner. Warren was born April 19, 1882, in Jersey City, NJ, the eldest son of Joseph Warren, a successful Jersey City real estate businessman born in Ireland, and his wife Ellen.

Initially hailed by Mayor Walker as the ideal man for the job, Warren's tenure was cut short after only 20 months, following a number of unsolved NYPD murder investigations, most notably including the highly publicized Arnold Rothstein murder investigation of November 1928.

In accepting Warren's resignation in December 1928, the mayor praised Warren as an honest public servant, but before he had even received Warren's resignation, he had already offered the office to Grover Whalen.

On the day he resigned, Warren was questioned in his office about whether he intended to quit. Warren pointed to the calendar on the wall of his office and noted that at 3 PM he would be in office for twenty months. The reporter asked if Warren made that observation because he intended to resign. Warren said, "No, I'm just pointing out that I lasted longer than McLaughlin."

Most people thought Mayor Walker was looking for a sensitive way to move Warren out of office when he noted that the strain of the job had adversely affected his friend's health. The mayor turned out to be correct when Warren was admitted to a sanitarium in Connecticut and succumbed to mental illness nine months later on August 13, 1929, an apparent victim to the rigors of his former office.[32]

During the relatively short period of time that the police department was under the command of commissioner's Mclaughlin and Warren they did not dismantle the police academy, nor did they expand its operations. There were, however, some operational changes made regarding how the academy conducted its business.

Under Commissioner McLaughlin, recruits no longer concluded the workday at 5 PM. Under the commissioner's new order, the recruits reported to the academy at 9 AM and for three hours were put through academic classes. At noon the recruits marched to the armory where they underwent an hour of military training and calisthenics. This was followed by three hours of down time that the recruits could use to study their academic topics. At 4 PM the recruits reported to assigned station houses in Manhattan and Brooklyn to begin four hours of pounding the pavement under the guidance of a veteran officer. The recruits wore no uniform but were armed with a revolver in case of an emergency. At 8 PM the recruits finally went off duty. When Friday night arrived the work week was no longer over. On Saturdays the recruits were required to report to the lieutenant in charge of the Detective Bureau for assignment to posts in front of banks, shops or manufacturing plants that handled amounts of money that would tempt crooks. Saturday evening the recruits reported back to the Detective Bureau to receive new posts, this time guarding theatres, places of amusement in the bright lights, and stores kept open for Saturday night shopping crowds.[33]

The Police College:

As far as training was concerned, Commissioner Grover Whalen basically inherited the same police academy put in place by Commissioner Enright, still under the command of Inspector John Noonan. The only difference was that it had been moved to a different location. The old Commerce Building on 23rd Street and Lexington Avenue officially closed its doors on November 1, 1926, forcing the police academy out with all the other occupants of the building.

Space was rented in the Grand Central Palace, a 13-story exposition hall located between 46th and 47th Streets. The Palace served as New York's main exposition hall from 1911 until 1953 when the exhibition space was replaced by office space for the Internal Revenue Service. The site served as a location for classrooms for the academy, while the physical training was conducted at the 69th and 71st Regiment Armories.

Whalen was born on July 2, 1886, in New York City, and was named after President Grover Cleveland. Whalen ran his father's ash and garbage disposal business for a time before becoming involved in politics, working for the election of John F. Hylan as Mayor of New York. After Hylan became Mayor in 1918, Whalen was appointed as Commissioner of Plants and Structures. In this position he supervised the city's transportation system. In 1924, Whalen left the Hylan administration to assist Rodman Wanamaker in the operation of the Wanamaker Department Stores, serving as general manager.

When it became clear that Commissioner Warren would have to go, Mayor Walker had to work quickly to identify a suitable replacement. Walker had a personal relationship with Grover Whalen and was aware of his administrative abilities when he was chairman of Walker's Reception Committee. Whalen was initially reluctant to accept the position because he was making more money at

Wannamaker's than he would as police commissioner. Jimmy Walker appealed to Whalen's responsibility to the Democratic party, and due to a feeling of civic responsibility and the fact that Walker helped to arrange a leave of absence for Whalen from Wannamaker's, he accepted the position.

Police Commissioner Whalen jumped into a wide range of changes in reorganizing the police department, but training was an area he took a special interest in. Whalen was impressed with the police academy established by Commissioner Enright, but he noted that the recruits were still receiving a pamphlet from 1914 called Police Practice and Procedure. All members of the force were required to keep the individual pamphlets in their possession and update them by hand as new orders were issued.

After studying the problem for several months Whalen replaced the pamphlets with a book called the Manual of Procedure, in which rules and regulations were correlated by subject matter. Every uniformed member of the force was given his own copy. Whalen explained that the new reference manual would eliminate indecision and doubt from the minds of members of the force and instill a feeling of confidence and tranquility in the conduct of official business.

In conjunction with the new rule book, Whalen set out to create the most modern and comprehensive police training program in the country. It would be an institution of higher learning like a college – a police college.

Commissioner Whalen summed up the need for modern training in commenting on the state of the city, "Whatever may be the causes of organized crime of today – its bold robberies, dastardly disregard for human life, in brief, its contempt for all the laws of society – the situation is critical."

Sound familiar? Almost a century ago New Yorkers were looking at out of control crime in the same way we view it today. There is one big difference, however. In the late 1920s the news media looked at the police as the solution the problem, as there was no defund the police campaign.

In 1929 New York City the police were looked upon as the bulwark against the "diabolical" minority responsible for the state of affairs in the city. There had been tremendous advances made from the police department in the 1890s. These advances came in many areas, but we will focus on the changes in police training. Even in 1929 the New York City Police Academy had been considered the most elaborate organization of any police school in the country. But to be the best in anything one cannot get complacent and rest on his laurels, so the New York City Police Department took a giant step forward in creating a Police College under Police Commissioner Grover Whalen. There were eleven schools within the college so it could just as easily been called the Police University.

Commissioner Whalen believed that crime control had to be approached from a scientific viewpoint as well as a practical one. Strong arm methods were alright in their place, but strong brain methods were equally important. Whalen realized the police had to outsmart the criminal or society would suffer. Crime had become so scientific that the police had to devise improved methods of approach to problems which formerly did not exist.

But how could Whalen's police college wage war against crime? The Commissioner pointed out that it was a prime essential that a detective had to have an excellent knowledge of the social foe with whom he was likely to deal. To that end the most experienced men in the department acquainted the new detectives with gangster manners and customs. He explained that it would take years to gain the knowledge which these hard-boiled detectives would impart in three months of intensive training at the Police College.

While the college was intended to make finer and broader minded policemen Commissioner Whalen cautioned that you must first have your policeman. Therefore, a large part of the building would be devoted to the rookie who was qualifying for the line of blue.

Candidates came from all over the country but a year's prior residence in New York was necessary. The candidate had to be under 29 years of age and weigh not less than 140 pounds. He had to pass rigid mental and physical examinations and was fingerprinted to make sure he was not a wolf in sheep's clothing.[34}

It didn't take long for the newspapers to begin getting a big laugh over the prospect of a college for policemen. This editorial was common for the time:

They will learn all the rules of catching criminals, but it would be just like the dirty crooks not to live up to the rules. Unless, of course, the crooks form a school of their own. If they do this, they could adopt as their college song "crash through the line of blue."

With educated cops and educated crooks, perhaps a sporting spirit will enter into arrests. The police may wait until the criminals call "Ready" before trying to catch them.

We suggest the following cheer for the police:
"Murderers, forgers, hold-up men,
They are the boys we put in the pen.
Rah, Rah, Rah,
Copper College, Copper College, Copper College."

Police Commissioner Whalen announced that Deputy Inspector John O'Connell would head the newly created Police College scheduled to open September 1, 1929. Inspector Noonan retained his current post and became O'Connell's assistant.

John O'Connell entered the police department in 1905. During the regime of Commissioner Enright, he was sent abroad for three months to study police conditions in Europe.[35]

On July 27, 1929, Whalen announced that the Sinking Fund Commission of the Board of Estimate had awarded an appropriation of $250,000 to rent Loft's old candy factory at Broome Street and

Cleveland Place, opposite the north end of Police Headquarters, on a five-year lease. The 8-story brick structure became the home of the Police College, the Police Engineer Bureau, and a garage for department vehicles.[36]

Fifty officers would comprise the Police College staff, but unlike the former police academy, these men would not be detached from their regular duties. Commissioner Whalen said the time given to the college would not interfere with their routine assignments and that the instructors would be glad to render this special service.

In addition to the staff of instructors, there would be an advisory council of three civilians who would serve without pay. The council would sit as a permanent board. Its first work would be to assign the instructors already selected to posts in the college for which they were best equipped. Many of the instructors selected were specialists in areas of police work like the detection of automobile thieves, pickpockets and confidence men, dealing with gang warfare, and handling traffic.

The first scheduled class would be conducted in the current police academy and was for new third grade detectives of the detective school. The course covered reports, court procedure and general lessons on the operations of thieves.[37]

Superintendent of Buildings Thomas O'Brien worked at getting the building in shape for the college which consisted of ten different units utilizing 17 classrooms. The new school was a radical departure from anything previously attempted; more comprehensive and varied, and the course for recruits would be at least twice as long as formerly. Instead of one class of fifty students, there would be several classes with smaller numbers of students all running at the same time.[38]

As the Police College began to take shape, three hundred probationary patrolmen of the New York City Police Department received diplomas at the police academy graduating exercise held at the 7th regiment Armory at Park Avenue and 66th Street in Manhattan.

The principal speaker was Mayor Jimmy Walker who told the men that the most dangerous thing to a patrolman was not the violent criminal but the power he holds and warned them that power was only to be used in emergencies and must never be misused.

Police Commissioner Whalen pointed out that the average patrolman in the class was 24 years 4 months old, weighed 162 ½ pounds and was 5 feet 9 ¾ inches in height. 275 of the men were born in the United States.[39]

More than five thousand people attended the graduation ceremony. Among the graduates was George Yamasheta, the first Japanese-American to join the department. There were 70% fewer Irish members than twenty years earlier. A decade later, in an action likely motivated by the treatment of Japanese-Americans at the start of Word War II, Patrolman George Yamasheta changed his name to George O'Connell. The graduation program was broadcast by stations WJZ and WNYC and the police band furnished music and dancing.[40]

Mayor Walker congratulated Inspector Noonan and declared that he wished the entire population of New York City could be present at a commencement of the Police Department College when it opened. Mayor Walker introduced Commissioner Whalen as the most popular executive New York City had ever had, and that he had always been a friend of the patrolmen.

It was easily the biggest night in the history of the police academy. A long and varied program was given by the men who had been trained under the supervision of Inspector Noonan. Calisthenics, marching, jiu-jitsu, and drilling were big features of the program which delighted the big audience. The evening parade of the graduates won a great deal of applause, as the men, in perfect rhythm, went around the floor of the armory.[41]

Although scheduled to open on September 1st, the Police College would not open until at least September 16th. The work of reconditioning the building progressed rapidly but was a bigger job than expected. The current police academy class was scheduled to move into the Police College building, but the condition of the building necessitated cancelling the move.[42]

Under the plan for the new Police College the policemen would be taught not only the methods of the criminal and the ways to circumvent his escape, but also how to deal more intelligently with the child or youth who committed minor offenses due to the influence of faulty environment or twisted personality. In these latter cases, the policemen, it was hoped, would be able to avoid recourse to arrest, but would substitute personal guidance or report the case to his superiors for handling by an agency other than the police, as for example, an organization such as an accredited Boy's Club or the Big Sisters.

In other instances, the policeman, through his training, if the plan was successful, would be able to recognize and report for appropriate action harmful influences that could be changed – dives catering to minors; evil family life; lack of play space, and similar causes of the first wrong step.

All this was intelligent, for it seemed logical for the police to interest themselves in siding healthy childhood in view of the fact that a majority of the more violent crimes had been shown to have been committed in recent years by persons from 18-26 years of age.

Meanwhile, it was, of course, the duty of the police to continue to strive for a higher percentage of arrests as compared to the number of crimes reported. It seemed likely all things being equal that trained men would be more successful in that, also, than officers turned out after haphazard study of a manual.[43]

With the opening of the new Police College the cop who relied on a strong arm and plenty of nerve had definitely taken his place among the relics of New York City's past. He and the valiant who years ago stepped off a boat to take a job on the force would have to put in a lot of schooling before they could get a job on the force in 1929. As it was,

60 percent of the newest recruits in the department had high school diplomas. Some of them were even trying for college degrees at night.

Most of the old timers wouldn't be able to fit their burly forms into the chairs the present patrolmen would occupy when they attended lectures. The corpulent arm of the law who was known as a "flatfoot" probably couldn't be dragged into a classroom to study crime.

The patrolman on the 1929 force would not go to the college immediately. The detectives would be the first to be subjected to the new process of education. After they had finished, the patrolmen would be taken in for a course.

There would be eleven schools in the new college under the direction of Deputy Inspector John J. O'Connell. In these schools, cops would learn everything from care of horses to the proper way to keep a filing cabinet. The most important and elaborate school in the college would be the school of law. Here the cop would be given thorough training in criminal law. He would learn how to build up evidence and how to present it as testimony.[44]

On October 7, 1929, the first sessions of the new Police College were held in the former Loft candy factory. No celebration marked the opening of the college as the official dedication would be held late in November, when all the college branches would be functioning. At that time there would be impressive ceremonies officiated by Mayor Walker.

Announcement of the opening of the college was made by Commissioner Whalen at a briefing in Police Headquarter. He said that 25-students comprising heads of detective divisions, attended the initial session of the detective school, at 10:30 AM, when Inspector Vincent Sweeney, who was an attorney, lectured on criminal law. Other lectures on the first day included criminal investigation and field methods, and Evidence.[45]

The Police College was the first institution of its kind in the world. It inaugurated a new policy of utilizing and advancing the arts and sciences underlying competent police work. As a place of learning it would rival many colleges where academic studies were pursued. The graduate, although he would not hold any scholastic degrees would nevertheless be well prepared for the intricate and ever-expanding duties of police work.

The police business of protecting society had become so complex and touched upon so many sides of specialized knowledge that it was important for the man on the force to have a thorough scientific preparation in addition to practical training. The Police College would differ from other institutions of learning, however, in that it would have for its students, men engaged in the very work which formed the subject of their study, and not immature youths as yet undecided as to what their special interest in later years would be.

The general plan of the college called for the operation of eleven separate schools:

- School of law
- School of officer training
- School of physical instruction
- School of motor and transportation
- School of horsemanship
- School of teachers' training
- School of traffic and safety
- School of aviation
- School of detective training
- School of specialized training
- School of recruit training

Instruction would include work in the physical sciences, sociology, psychology, detective administration, criminology, advanced law, evidence, statistics, ballistics, advanced criminal identification and investigation, and other sciences related to police service. Every form of evil doing, from shooting to poisoning and from larceny to bomb throwing would be studied. The medical aspects of crime, its mechanical aids and appliances, the methods of the racketeer, gunman, safe-blower, professional thief, drug addict, and other malefactors would be covered.

Divergent criminal types and factors underlying the geographical distribution of criminals and the nature and technique of their organization would be analyzed. The theory method, by which a detective sets out to solve a crime on the basis of hypothesis, would be abandoned in favor of the more useful orientation method where every step was dictated by the correlation of known facts.

Along with the general progress of society, the advance of crime and the greater resourcefulness of the criminal had been noted. The malefactor made use of the latest scientific aids. To cope with the modern criminal the police had to be equally keen and with equal knowledge. The paramount object, therefore, was to increase the efficiency and crime detecting ability of the uniformed and plainclothes units of the police force. Criminal investigation required not only a high degree of intelligence on the part of the investigating officers, but intelligence supported by courage, tact, energy and extensive acquaintance with human nature, as well as with all branches of the law, according to the theory of the school.

The establishment of a Police College was attributed to the recognition of the changing conditions under which the police worked. Criminology was a specialized profession, no longer the happy hunting ground of adventurous spirits with a disinclination for socially useful and sustained effort. The comparative youth of the American police was regarded as the cause of some of their shortcomings in the past.[46]

Faced with an entirely different modus operandi on the part of the underworld from that against which it matched its wits decades earlier, the Police Department was seeking to evolve a new type of policeman through the Police College which began classes for third grade detectives and squad commanders in the old Loft Candy Building, directly opposite Police Headquarters.

Racketeering, a type of crime unknown a few years earlier, and "big business" methods in fur thefts and the disposal of stolen goods, were among the latest ramifications of the underworld against which the police department was training its shock troops of "college cops."

Dr. William Grady, District Superintendent of the Board of Education and a member of the committee of four educators appointed by Police Commissioner Whalen to make a study of the curriculum at the Police College and to suggest improvements on the course in criminology, did not, however, want the impression to get abroad that the department was turning out "collegiate" policemen.

"Don't think for a minute that we're trying to transform the policemen into collegiate graduates," he said during a speech. "Our slogan is to take the curse of the academic from these courses."

Institutions similar to the Police College were started during the regimes of Commissioners Woods and Enright but were discontinued. Dr. Grady said, "the failure of similar institutions in earlier administrations was the stimulus for this new and better type of police training school. The general philosophy back of this innovation is this. Business of all kinds found that it increases its efficiency to educate its personnel to a wider vision and broader knowledge, the Police Department is a modern business, and its competitor is the underworld."[47]

The first non-detectives to enter the Police College were 29 sergeants and 30 patrolmen, all in line for promotions. They were temporarily assigned to the Police College to pursue a five-week course in the officers' training division on the duties of lieutenant and sergeant of police. The men were relieved of their precinct duties and devoted all of their time in familiarizing themselves with the duties of the next higher rank to which they hoped to be advanced to in a short time.[48]

Men of the NYPD were not the only members of the department receiving training at the Police College. Women in the NYPD go all the way back to 1845 when the first female jail matrons were hired.

Legislation was enacted to appoint female police matrons in 1888, and the first four were hired in 1891. Matrons were responsible for the care of the station house and the women and children held there. They tended to be working-class women, and many were widows with a family connection to policing.

In the 1900s and 1910s, some matrons were assigned to detective squads to conduct investigative work. Although they often officially retained the "matron" rank and salary, contemporary newspapers and court records frequently referred to them as "policewomen", "police officers", and "detectives".

In 1921, the Women's Police Precinct was formed with 20 patrolwomen assigned, however it closed shortly after in 1923. In 1924, the New York Police Department's Women Bureau was created.

In 1934, female officers began to have pistol practice with male officers and in 1938, the first civil service exam for the title "Policewoman" was given.

In 1942, there began a requirement of a college degree for female officers and in 1958 women and men began to train together at the Police Academy.

In 1970, the first woman was allowed to take the test for Police Administrative Aides, and the first women were hired from the Police Administrative List. Also in that year, Police Commissioner Murphy assigned the first group of women to patrol. In 1973, the Bureau of Policewomen was abolished, and the first gender-neutral civil service exam for police officers was held. Also in that year, "Policewomen" and "Patrolmen" were officially renamed "Police Officers".

Back at the Police College, Inspector Noonan had a problem. 45 females were present to begin training, but he wasn't sure of their job titles. How could the head of the Police College not know who was being trained? It was a tale that went back to Commissioner Enright's first year in office when the titles of both "policewoman" and "patrolwoman" were established.

Each job title was sure that it was more important and of higher rank than the other though the salaries were the same, the requirements almost identical and both were subject to assignment by the commissioner or his inspectors to any police duty that was needed within the "women's sphere."

Inspector Noonan, when asked about the difference between a patrolwoman and a policewoman said, "It took me seven weeks to find out and I'm not sure I know yet."

One difference was gleaned from the physical requirements for application. Patrolwoman applicants had to be at least 5 feet 2 inches tall, have a minimum weight of 120 pounds and be between the ages of 21 and 35 years of age. Policewomen applicants had to be at least 5 feet 4 inches tall, be between the ages of 30 and 40, and present a statement signed by 20 or more women residents of New York City in good standing to the effect that the applicant was "suitable for the position." Both policewomen and patrolwomen started at the patrolmen's salary of $1,769 with yearly increases up to the maximum.

Another difference that was not generally known was that policewomen were eligible for the police pension and paid in 2 percent of their salaries to the police pension fund just as patrolmen did. They were also held strictly under civil service rules. Patrolwomen were not civil service employees, and although they paid into the regular city pension fund were not eligible for the police pension. That didn't seem very fair.

Both policewomen and patrolwomen appealed to the Legislature that the women be formed into a definite platoon of the police department with graded ranks such as were enjoyed by the men but denied the women. While their demand for rank structure was similar, one side demanded that everybody be called patrolwoman and the other held that policewoman was the only title worth having.

The policewomen had the advantage of numbers and the backing of the Civil Service Commission, and the power of an association of their own. The patrolwomen lost their chief sponsor with the retirement of Enright who was responsible for their origin. The women in both titles entering the Police College were there to take an intensive course in training for their jobs of one month.

One of the duties often assigned to policewomen in Brooklyn and Manhattan was to raid certain public places for "mashers" In preparation for handling any such person who may prove obstreperous when arrested the women were taught jiu-jitsu.

These women at the Police College made application for the job several months earlier giving their education, experience and physical data. If these were satisfactory, they were called for an examination by the Civil Service Commission. They were given first a physical examination, both medical and athletic. They had to chin the bar, do the dip which is to show the strength of their body muscles; jump over a rope at least three feet high, and do other physical exercises to show that they were supple and strong. Their feet were examined and their legs to their knees. Every possible precaution was taken to weed out the women who were not physically equal to the duties of handling prisoners, caring for children or doing some of the unpleasant things that came all too often into the life of a policewoman.

If they got by the physical examination, the women were called for a mental test. This included general questions on their duties, opinions as to various methods of combatting crime, geography of the city, location of amusement places where their duties might be expected to lead them, theories for meeting given emergency conditions and other matters directly connected to their jobs. The questions were so planned that the women's originality of thought, quickness of perception, judgement and humanitarian attitude were brought out. The general education was tested by the appearance of spelling, penmanship and the wording of papers.

When all the testing was completed – and it had to be done within a specified period of time – the candidates were rated. If a rating of 70 percent was gained in all the subjects the policewoman was placed on the eligible list to await appointment to the first vacancy. The 25 who were in the Police College passed all the stages and then had to face the test of the Police College where they had to prove that they were as well equipped for the job as their previous examinations seemed to show.

Inspector Noonan was very enthusiastic over the women's class and expressed great satisfaction over the high standard of women who had come to the Police College.

The women each were given a shield of which they were very proud. They were not given the same physical instruction as the men for the claim was that they did not need it in their work. They wore no uniforms, although Inspector Noonan said, "I hope someday that we will have uniformed policewomen in the parks. I feel they could be very useful in preventing vandalism."

The women learned just enough of the art of self-defense to be able to handle a prisoner without violence. At the Women's Bureau at Police Headquarters the statement was made that "If a policewoman cannot handle a prisoner without violence, she has no business on the force." But the women got none of the thrills of horsemanship, boxing, hurdle jumping and other sports that men adored, and which did so much to make the city cops deserve the title of the finest.

There was also another fly in the ointment of the policewoman. Mrs. Mary Hamilton was the head of the 13th Division, popularly known as the Woman's Bureau, and certain women were assigned to her department including at least one woman in each borough who looked to her bureau for orders. Other women, however, were assigned to the police stations to do the work of a matron or to special divisions for special duty concerning women and children. These women were not technically under the direction of Mrs. Hamilton, and they instantly resented the statement of the Woman's Bureau that all women in the police department were under the Woman's Bureau. These specially assigned women drew their pay from the stations or divisions to which they were assigned and disclaimed strenuously any connection with the Women's Bureau. Just why there was this strong objection to being counted in the 13th Division was not clear, but the feeling was there 100 percent.

The policewomen and patrolwomen reporting to Inspector Noonan at the Police College were certainly not treated as equals to the men on the department, but there had been many positive changes for the women over the prior thirty years. Only eight years earlier, policewomen worked ten to fourteen hours a day with 24-hours every other Sunday at a salary of $1000 a year. After graduating from the Police College, they would serve in three shifts of 8 hours. The first policewoman had the rank of doorman and the salary of patrolman. When the rank of doorman was abolished, the women were left without salary or status, so legislature created the rank of policewoman.

One more grievance existed at that time. The women who were policemen's widows were given the job of bedmaker in the stations, but they were not policewomen until they passed the necessary examinations. Their status as widows did not help one bit in applying for policewoman. But the belief was general that policewomen were preferably widows of policemen.[49]

In an attempt to continue the momentum of the new Police College, an appropriation of $10,000 to be used in promoting the scientific phases of policework was requested from the Board of Estimate. Police Commissioner Whalen announced that half the money would go to retain a pathologist to work with the homicide squad while the rest would provide lectures in criminology.[50]

Even though the Police College was off to a flying start, the concept of the training school was not universally accepted. Applying the fundamentals of big business to an organization founded on militaristic principles brought more adverse criticism against Grover Whalen than anything else. And when the New York Police

Commissioner announced he would establish a college in an old candy factory devoted entirely to police work, the citizenry scoffed openly.

Many of the scoffers went to the former candy factory for the formal dedication of the facility. And when they had inspected the world's first police college, most went away singing its praises.

Although the eight-story building and its equipment which comprised the new Police College was dedicated in December, the school itself had been in operation since October. An enormous staff headed by Deputy Inspector John J. O'Connell, had been conducting classes for three months. The Police College building was officially designated as the Police Department Annex. On the 8th floor was a huge cafeteria, seating 500. Food for members of the force was sold at cost price. On the second floor was an auditorium for special lectures and entertainments.

While the members of O'Connell's faculty were almost entirely recruited from the police force, the system was planned so as to guard against inefficiency in organization. An advisory board of leading educators consulted frequently with the active faculty members so that police instructors could not fail to address important issues. The curriculum covered courses for raw recruits on the force to post-graduate work for men who had advanced to high positions in the Police Department.

There were 29 classrooms to accommodate 2100 embryo and active members of New York's Finest. Of the eight floors in the large building, each with a floor space of 15,000 square feet, three were devoted entirely to the actual college (4th 5th and 6th). Each classroom was well lighted, heated, ventilated, and equipped with approximately 50 tablet armchairs and blackboards. Portable projectoscopes were also available.

There were 11 classroom units on the 4th floor. The Motor Transport School was equipped for men in the automotive service. The types of machines used for police work were displayed. Actual shop and laboratory supplemented academic training. Another unit on this floor was assigned to the School of Horsemanship. Candidates for the mounted service received all the theoretical training in the building while the actual riding is done at the Police Horsemanship School at Sheepshead Bay. On this floor also was a model muster room of a police station house containing the latest equipment for quick dispatch of police information, reports on crimes, and methods of signaling and recall. Then there was also the complete light signal system for the control of traffic.

There were 11 classroom units on the 5th floor in addition to a comprehensive library on criminology, sociology, psychology, police methods, etc., as well as textbooks and manuals. The library was open to student recruits and all members of the force.

The 6th floor had seven classroom units. Also, on this floor was perhaps the most unique museum of its kind in the world. It was a complete crime museum featuring almost everything connected with crime and police work. There was for instance, in one cabinet all the exhibits used by the prosecution in the famous Snyder-Gray murder case. Another interesting exhibit included counterfeit money and all the paraphernalia required to turn out spurious currency.

Thus had Grover Whalen launched the most elaborate of "new-fangled" ideas in police service – and, in the opinion of prominent educationalists who attended the dedication, a monument to a man who refused to run the city's police force on the lines of old school club-wielding patrolmen and raucous voiced sergeants.[51]

Police Commissioner Whalen appeared to be in the role of college president when, with President Joseph McKee of the Board of Aldermen and most members of that body, he reviewed the graduation exercises of the Police College at Police Headquarters. The comprehensive exercises included calisthenics, marching, boxing, leg gymnastics, exhibitions in class and mat jiu-jitsu, rifle practice.

Despite the absence of caps and gowns the atmosphere was distinctly collegiate and most of the speeches bore an academic aspect. "This institution was established to bring the scientific developments of the age to the attention of policemen who here receive their higher education. We are trying to raise this work from the level of an occupation to that of a profession," said Commissioner Whalen.[52]

Less than a week after the graduation, some of the "glow" emanating from the Police Commissioner's newly opened Police College began to slightly dim when it was discovered that the building had been robbed.

The electric lights were taken from their sockets, and paper cutters, used to open the "fan" mail to recruits were pilfered. New security protocols were immediately instituted to keep better control of all persons entering the building. The result was that the facility was made exclusive to members of the police department with visitors required to obtain a pass before being allowed entry.

Discussing the looting, Whalen noted that the public was permitted to eat lunch in the cafeteria on the 8th floor, and many such diners took advantage to stock up on lamps and other knick-knacks. "It reminds me of the time when I was Commissioner of Plant and Structures," said Whalen. "We ran the ferryboats and commuters stole everything but the smokestacks."[53]

It wasn't long before the impact of the Police College was felt outside New York City. Two instructors in the Police College were loaned to the city of Houston, Texas, to reorganize the police department there. This loan of personnel was the result of a visit to the Police College by Houston Mayor Walter E. Monteith and Chief of Police William C. McPhail, who immediately after the visit made application for the loan of two instructors to train 300 members of the Houston police force.[54]

As time passed, much to the chagrin of a segment of the police department, Commissioner Whalen continued in his quest to merge the Police College into an actual institution of higher learning. His target for this goal was the New York State Board of Regents.

The Regents are responsible for general supervision of all educational activities within New York State, presiding over the State University and the New York State Educational Department. Commissioner Whalen was understandably excited at the end of January in 1930 when he wined and dined the Regents of the University of the State of New York at the Bankers' Club in Manhattan. Following lunch Whalen conducted a tour of Police Headquarters and the Police College.[55] The Board of Regents departed the Police College with a big request to consider. Commissioner Whalen requested that graduates of the Police College receive diplomas with the hallmark of the State Board of Regents.[56]

In life, timing is everything. At the same time that Commissioner Whalen was making his push to have the Police College recognized by the Board of Regents, the Baumes Bill was submitted to the New York State Legislature. If this bill authored by State Senator Caleb H. Baumes and Burton D. Esmond was successful, all members of police departments in New York State would be required to take promotional examinations that were approved by the Board of Regents, which would establish standards of instruction and charter all the police schools. In other words, The State Board of Education would have complete control over all police examinations.

At first glance, it would seem that the timing of the Baumes Bill was perfect in joining with Commissioner Whalen's efforts with the Board of Regents, but the reality was quite different. Segments of the police department, the newspaper media, and the public, began to look at the initiatives as an attempt to turn the police department into a college campus. These sentiments were expressed in an article in the Times Union.

"We want no state managed colleges, with the regents conducting the examinations," declared a well-known police official. "The men are

perfectly satisfied with the present methods of examination and promotions, and they do not want to get a college spirit, other than the one now in vogue. First thing you know they would be wearing wide trousers, go without hats, play ukuleles and sing college songs – Let the police alone."[57]

The Brooklyn Daily Eagle got right to the point regarding their feelings about college education for police officers.

Most of us think some degree should be devised by the State Regents for the graduates of Commissioner Whalen's Police College. Let us suggest M.C. Master of Clubs. Clubs are always trumps in police work.[58]

Of course, there was also patronage in the Baumes Bill. An inspector of police training would be created with a number of assistants, as many as the Board of Regents deem advisable, as warranted by the amount of money appropriated.[59]

Brooklyn used the attempts to get the Board of Regents involved with police training to further its own agenda. Ever since the consolidation of the Greater City of New York in 1898 Brooklyn had suffered from something of an inferiority complex. Many in Brooklyn had been against the consolidation, referring to it as "the great mistake of 98." They resented that their great city, which had been third largest in the nation, was folded into a borough withing New York City. Brooklynites favored themselves more intelligent and less corrupt than their neighbors across the river who had been ruled for years by the corrupt politicians in Tammany Hall.

In 1930, Einstein's Theory of Relativity and the fourth dimension were in the news. In fact, there was a debate about including Einstein's theory in the elementary school curriculum.

One Brooklyn newspaper took a swipe at the intellectual capabilities of Manhattanites while bringing the Police College into the fray.

Relativity, if certain political reforms can be sold to the Committee of the Whole of the Board of Estimate will soon be taught in this borough's elementary schools. When certain of Brooklyn's political leaders, corpulent and otherwise, sought to have relativity and a knowledge of the fourth dimension made a requirement for graduates of the Police College, why do you think Tammany voted solidly against it? They knew that if the measure was passed only Brooklyn boys would be admitted to the force. They would have to admit that Mayor Walker, and Commissioner Whalen do not comprehend the fourth dimension.

The inference in the article was that only Brooklyn police recruits would be smart enough to comprehend the Theory of Relativity, and that even the Mayor and Police Commissioner weren't intelligent enough to understand the fourth dimension. By the way, for those of you like me, who don't know what the fourth dimension is, according to Einstein, you need to describe where you are not only in three-dimensional space – length, width, and height – but also in time. Time is the fourth dimension.[60]

In April of 1930 the agenda of Commissioner Whalen's Police College was still moving forward with recruit graduations being events filled with more pomp and circumstance than ever before. Under the approving eyes of Mayor Walker and Police Commissioner Whalen 527 rookie patrolmen, members of the graduating class of the Police College, went through their drills and exercises in Madison Square Garden and received their diplomas. The commencement exercises marked the end of a three-month period of intensive training. With the conclusion of the exercises the graduates became full-fledged New York policemen. The band of the police, fire and Sanitation departments provided the music for the drills and the review by Commissioner Whalen and Mayor Walker, and for the dancing which followed the exercises. The speeches by the Mayor and Police Commissioner were broadcast over station WEAF and the National Broadcasting System.[61]

Another forum for Commissioner Whalen to showcase his Police College was the annual Police Parade. From 1857 to 1934 the police department held an annual parade to put on public display their military deportment, professionalism, equipment, and recent innovations of the force, such as new uniforms and new units. The parade also provided a forum to present medals to the men who earned them for acts of heroism and valor performed the prior year. Medals earned by officers killed in the line of duty were presented to surviving relatives. The public loved the parades as thousands lined the parade route to watch New York's Finest march by.

In 1930 Mayor Walker and Commissioner Whalen presided over the greatest police parade the city has ever had. It was an outstanding spectacle of pageant that was all color and brilliance. The theme of the parade was the contrast between "yesterday" and "today" as some members of the department marched under the banner of the Old Broadway Squad, decked out in the uniform of the 1890s, complete with knee length coats, great badges, long sticks stuck in their bulging belts, bean pot hats, and yes, brave and bristling moustaches. They strutted down Fifth Avenue amid a burst of applause, the more appreciated because the uniforms contrasted greatly with the very modern uniforms worn by their brother officers.

The parade included the impressive ceremony of pinning the gold stars on the department flag, in memory of the men who died during the past year while on duty. It was done by Commissioner Whalen, and when he finished, a patrolman standing at his elbow blew taps. Then, from far up 5th Avenue came another "taps" as if to echo it. It was fitting that the beautiful ceremony should come after thirteen medals of honor were given to the men living who had earned them for bravery.

The boys from the Police College were a big hit too. Thousands of people watching must have rubbed their eyes and questioned if they were watching the police parade as the columns of singing young college boys came into sight. Their dress for the parade was not the conventional blue and brass buttons. No, they were typically collegiate in white ducks, open-throat gray jerseys and tricky little berets perched on the back of their heads. They swung their arms and sang loud and cheerily the beer song that had put the University of Maine on the map. The song was officially called The Maine Stein Song, and had been around since 1902, but in 1930 Rudy Vallée recorded the song with a faster tempo and a few word changes. The song topped the charts for two months and was the leading song of the year. It became the only college song to become a number one hit. Some of the lyrics are as follows:

Oh, fill the steins to dear old Maine
Shout till the rafters ring
Stand and drink a toast once again
Let every loyal Maine man sing
Then drink to all the happy hours
Drink to the careless days
Drink to Maine, our alma mater
The college of our hearts always
To the trees, to the sky, to the Spring and its glorious happiness
To the youth, to the fire, to the light that is moving and calling us
To the gods, to the fate, to the rulers of men and their destinies
To the lips, to the eyes, to the girls who will love us someday [62]

Meanwhile, the advancements in modern police training continued at the Police College. Outfitted with all the impediments of the modern crook or gangster, a dummy gunman was put into use at the Police College to show recruit officers the tricks of the criminal. The dummy was a veritable arsenal of weapons, pistols, knives, saws, and blackjacks hidden about the clothing and every place the ingenious crook might choose, to demonstrate to the students that a cursory frisk was not always safe. The dummy also wore a bullet proof vest.[63]

Proponents of the Police College found its work fascinating to the extreme. One of the most interesting and important branches of the work was that taken care of by the motor transport school for men in the automotive service. More than 1,800 men were registered for instruction in this school. Instruction covered much more than care of the department automobiles. Everything that should be known about the handling of the equipment and the repairs necessary was taught the men who took the course.

The course of instruction covered ten weeks, 3.5 hours each week. During this time the department cars were taken apart and reassembled. Lectures on each component part, making very clear the functions that each part must fill in the operation and performance of the car, were given. Motion pictures were used extensively to illustrate roadside repairs and every instruction period was followed by an open discussion based upon the actual parts that were on exhibition in the classroom.

The Chrysler Corporation, which supplied 12 Chrysler "70" sedans was cooperating by assigning trained men to instruct the classes in the proper and economical handling of their cars. Every detail of the cars was explained to the various classes by those men who lectured by means of drawings thrown upon the screen in the lecture room. Equipment placed at the disposal of the police department by the Chrysler Corporation was most helpful according to police officials.[64]

The End:

Everything was going as well as Commissioner Whalen could have hoped for regarding his Police College until a problem developed – a big problem. Whalen came under fire for the police handling of the International Unemployment Day demonstration on March 6, 1930, in New York City, in which an impromptu march of 35,000 or more demonstrators down Broadway to New York City Hall was set upon by 1,000 baton-wielding police.

The brutal scene was described by a reporter from the New York Times:

"Hundreds of policemen and detectives, swinging nightsticks, blackjacks, and bare fists, rushed into the crowd, hitting out at all with whom they came into contact, chasing many across the street and into adjacent thoroughfares and pushing hundreds off their feet. From all parts of the scene of battle came the screams of women and cries of men with bloody heads and faces."

Sharply criticized for the escalation of violence by the police, Whalen was forced to resign his post within two months.

Incoming Police Commissioner Edward P. Mulrooney was the direct antithesis of Grover Whalen. Mulrooney had risen from within the ranks of the NYPD and was more publicity-shy than a modest violet, as opposed to Whalen who enjoyed being on the front page of every newspaper every day during his 17-month tenure as police commissioner.

Mulrooney went about his life with a quiet determination since he began working with his father on a tugboat in 1896. He had just obtained his pilot's license when he saw an advertisement in a newspaper, signed by Police Commissioner Theodore Roosevelt, asking healthy young men to join the police force. The rest was history.[65]

After his conference with incoming Commissioner Mulrooney, Whalen believed Mulrooney would continue the Police College with Whalen as honorary president. Whalen's optimism was bolstered by an interview Mulrooney conducted with a reporter.

The reported asked, "Will you continue most of Commissioner Whalen's policies?"

"I will." Mulrooney replied. He further declared that he did not contemplate any sweeping changes, and that the police work would continue uninterrupted by any wholesale reorganization.[66]

In an official farewell to the force Whalen issued an order giving every member of the department one day's additional vacation as recognition of faithful service. Whalen returned to Wannamaker's to resume the executive post he occupied before being appointed police commissioner.[67]

Whalen's belief that the Police College would continue appeared to be justified when Commissioner Mulrooney added to the Police College staff with the addition of the first prosecutor to join the faculty. Queens Assistant District Attorney Konowitz, of Jamaica was appointed instructor in criminal law, procedure and evidence on the recommendation of District Attorney John Hallinan. This was the first time a district attorney's office was asked to participate at the Police College. The Queens prosecutor would be attached to the school of detectives, and his class would hold 70 sleuths from all over the city.[68]

Another new addition to the Police College occurred when 28-students were instructed in cutting through steel with acetylene torches under the supervision of Sergeant William Reuboldt of the Hunters Point Emergency Squad and Sergeant William McMahon of the Police College.[69]

As the new year of 1931 began there was no reason to think that the Police College would do anything but continue its advance as the preeminent police training school as well as an institute of higher learning. But on January 9th Police Commissioner Mulrooney received a call that changed everything. The call was from Dr. Frank Graves, President of the University of the State of New York and State Commissioner of Education. Dr. Graves explained that for an educational institution to qualify as college it must have an endowment of at least $500,000 and must observe certain standards including a high school education, as qualifications for admission as a student. It must also have a four-year course.

Commissioner Mulrooney conceded that recruits did not need a high school diploma to enter Police College, and that the recruits training was for three months, not four years. The Commissioner also said that there was no endowment for the Police college.

Dr. Graves said that since the Police College did not meet the requirements to be considered a college, its name must be changed to remove "college" from its title. With a stroke of Commissioner Mulrooney's pen, the Police College was cast into the ash heap of history and the Police Academy was reborn.[70]

The name may have changed, but the building and function was the same. One of Commissioner Mulrooney's pet police academy projects came to fruition during the summer of 1931.

The bewildered visitor to the city standing in the Grand Central area and looking hopefully at the city's indifference found himself accosted by blue uniforms covering courtly hearts when Police Commissioner Mulrooney's special courtesy patrolmen – his "ambassadors of the city" – went on duty.

According to a description in a newspaper, this squad was composed of 84 of the tallest and handsomest June 1931 graduates of the Police College / Academy. They would be an auxiliary to the regular force, similar to the Coldstream Guards and the Royal Horse of His Majesty's forces in England.

The new squad members were between 22 and 26 years old and between 5 feet 10 ½ inches and 6 feet 4 ½ inches tall, and they had just completed a ten-day courtesy course under Inspector John O'Connell of the Police Academy.

O'Connell explained, "The patrolmen who comprise the new detail were specially selected and trained to deal courteously and efficiently with the problems presented by tourists. The section of the city which will be in the particular charge of the detachment is the center of both business and amusement activities. It is the part of the city in which New York visitors who average more than one million daily spend the major portion of their time and on which their impressions of the metropolis as whole are based."

The official range of the squad was from Sixth Avenue to Lexington Avenue from 34th to 60th Streets. It had no station house of its own and worked from 8 AM to 5 PM.[71]

Things went on as usual in the big 8-story building on Broome Street. Even though the "Police College" title hadn't been used in over three years, the police academy still went about the business of turning recruits into police officers and providing specialized training to all members of the department. It seemed like a small detail that the five-year lease on the Broome Street building was set to expire. After all, the plan was for the city to purchase the building. That plan, however, was derailed when Manhattan Borough President Samuel Levy, sole Tammany member of the Board of Estimate, shot down the plan to buy the Police Department Annex at a private sale for $495,000.

Comptroller Joseph D. McGoldrick had offered the resolution to buy the property, which was still owned by Loft, Inc., Candy Makers. Mr. Levy immediately produced affidavits showing that the owners of the building, when they applied for a reduction of assessed valuation, valued the building at only $250,000. The appraisal at that figure was made by an examiner for the Emigrant Industrial Bank. The building carried an assessed valuation of $515,000 and had been leased for the last five years at $65,000 a year.[72]

The other big problem was Fiorello Henry La Guardia. The 99th Mayor of New York City entered office in 1934. Known for his irascible, energetic, and charismatic personality and diminutive, rotund stature, La Guardia is acclaimed as one of the greatest mayors in American history.

In 1934 the country was still in the throes of the Great Depression, and La Guardia came to office with his main goals being to restore financial health and end corruption in government. Mayor LaGuardia was tired of millions of dollars of private property being unloaded on the city for public purposes at fancy prices far in excess of real value. The mayor demonstrated in no uncertain manner his attitude toward this sort of thing by his action in the case of the property on Broome Street.

Said the mayor: "I am sick and tired of these false appraisals going before the courts and the courts making believe that they don't know anything about values. They've placed the value of their building by their own appraisers at $250,000. Now let's see them squirm out."

Following an inspection tour by Mayor LaGuardia the purchase idea was given up and in addition the mayor ordered the building vacated by the end of the month when the lease expired. Quarters were found in other city buildings. The mayor declared that all property being used by the city would be treated in the same way from then on.[73]

With all the appearance of an eviction hundreds of police and city workers struggled to remove the assorted paraphernalia and equipment of the once proud Police College, as the department moved to abandon the building on Broome Street. Every station house in the city was ordered to make room for the miscellaneous equipment ranging from ink wells to emergency trucks. The basement of Police Headquarters was used for the Property Clerk's office and the printing plant, while the thousands of files of the department were shifted to the old Sheriff Street station.[74]

The Police College name and building were not the only staples of the institution that were abandoned. Acting Deputy Chief John Noonan, who for many years had overseen the training of many thousands of new policemen, was forced to retire because of his age.[75]

The Police Academy was forced to move across the river to cramped quarters on the upper floors of the grey, brick 84th Precinct on Poplar Street, within the shadow of the Brooklyn Bridge. Still sporting their inferiority complex, Brooklyn wasted no time in declaring itself the leader in police education.

Inspector O'Connell moved his many activities into the Poplar Street precinct house on September 1st. Determined not to curtail the activities of his academy despite the cramped quarters, O'Connell had ordered his men to prepare a room for the college's famed crime museum – one of the weirdest collections ever compiled. Additionally, the Police Academy began conducting classes for elementary school teachers in accident reduction and crime prevention. More than 1200 elementary school teachers and 400 parochial schoolteachers graduated from the program. Because of the limited space at Poplar Street, the teachers received their training at the City College building on 23rd Street in Manhattan.

Due to the success of the program, the academy instituted classes for high school teachers. The elementary school teachers would attend classes on Mondays and Wednesdays and were taught how to organize safety patrols and fire prevention. The secondary instructors were lectured on such weightier subjects as physical and mental causes of accidents and traffic engineering. At the end of each term the teachers were required to pass an examination and the studious ones received credits which resulted in higher pay.

Inspector O'Connell had the brawny body of a policeman and the head and mind of a dean. He had traveled throughout the world studying police crime prevention methods and there was not a major city in the United States he had not visited on official business. He joined the department as a patrolman, following graduation from LaSalle Military Academy and served in practically every branch of the department during his long service. He was a detective for 14 years, a captain in charge of the Jamaica precinct, a captain in charge of the very busy West 47th Street station, and an inspector in charge of the uniformed forces on the East side of Manhattan.

In commenting about the program to instruct teachers, O'Connell said, "You must reach the children in school for effective correction. Often, I'm walking with my own youngsters, and they'll stop me at a corner and say, 'Daddy, wait for the traffic lights.' They learned that in school."[76]

The Legacy of the Police College:

Police Commissioner Whalen's Police College was gone, but the legacy of the police department's association with colleges was just beginning. In the meantime, the police academy struggled through two decades of inadequate facilities. The Poplar Street academy was terribly cramped, and in 1946 the Board of Estimate notified the police department that an abandoned school building on Manhattan's Lower West Side, just released by the Army, would be turned over to the department for conversion into a police academy.

Work on the five-story building on Hubert and Collision Streets began immediately so that the training school could be moved from the overburdened Poplar Street location as soon as possible. Quick action was necessary because 24,000 candidates took the most recent police civil service examination and the department had over 3,000 positions to fill. The Poplar Street academy could handle only 250 recruits in a class.

The improvement at Hubert Street was minimal at best. Academy operations continued to be handicapped at the antiquated, decrepit 19th century abandoned schoolhouse that one officer described as almost fit for human habitation.

During the 1950s the situation had deteriorated to the point that the NYPD Annual Report described recruit training as follows:

Recruits must divide their training time between a condemned public school building in Manhattan, ten pistol ranges scattered throughout the city, and physical training at the New York City pavilion in Flushing Meadow Park in Queens, or an armory at Bedford and Atlantic Avenues in Brooklyn.

1954 Police Annual Report [77]

No matter how dismal the physical facilities of the police academy became, the light of the high ideals of the Police College continued to flicker. The history of the New York City Police Department and the municipal colleges can be traced to the 1920s when the CCNY School of Business began offering in-service training courses to New York City policemen. In 1954, a plan to affiliate the Baruch School with the police academy was announced by Mayor Robert F. Wagner.

The plan would include an inter-change of instructors, with police trainees taking courses with civilian teachers, and Baruch students with seasoned police instructors.

Police Commissioner Francis P. Adams proposed an eventual placement of the police training school in a new $3,800,000 building adjacent to the Baruch School. The commissioner said, "We are trying to raise the level of police training to a higher professional standing," and asserted that the new program would attract new members to the police department.[78]

The Police Science Program at Baruch School of Business and Public Administration of City College emphasized a strong liberal arts curriculum as the basis of a sound police education. Over the next decade, the program grew substantially, attracting large numbers of students. For the first time, courses offered to students at the police academy who wished to earn the Associate in Applied Science degree were available.[79] And soon after the program was extended to admit personnel from all other law enforcement agencies.

The college level training program offering intensive professional training for law enforcement officers, was enthusiastically attended by members of the force from the rank of patrolman to inspector. Expanding this program by admitting other law enforcement agencies was in line with the department policy of fostering the principles of professionalism in the police field.

The program offered courses in English composition and literature, public speaking, human relations, American Government, sociology, criminology, law and science, as well as police organization, supervision, administration, principles of investigation and juvenile delinquency.

The Baruch program proved reasonably successful with enrollment increasing from 600 police officers in 1957 to 1,204 by 1964. Cramped classrooms and deteriorating buildings, however, stifled the program. Additionally, pressure was building both in New York City and nationally to expand police education.[80]

In 1957 Mayor Wagner received approval for a new police academy and ground was finally broken in April 1960 for the new 8-story, state-of-the-art training facility located on East 20th Street in Manhattan.[81]

The new police academy was expected to be completed during 1962, but construction on the $8 million facility was set back at least a year by strikes of the concrete and iron workers.[82]

The work continued well beyond an additional year and $8 million had grown to $10 million, but finally on August 31, 1964 the new police academy was dedicated by Mayor Wagner. Although completed later than expected and with more expense, the new academy was impressive. A tour of the 8-story education and training plant with three basements showed how the vision had been realized in terms of a first-floor corridor with glass and Vermont marble walls, a swimming pool, sparkling research laboratories, a rooftop drill field, a television production studio, and other stuff of which police officials' dreams were made of.[83]

During the new police academy dedication ceremony, Mayor Wagner said that New York City continued to be the nation's leader in progressive police thinking and modern law enforcement. The structure, which also housed the 13th precinct, the police lab, medical bureau and museum was officially turned over to Police Commissioner Michael J. Murphy by Public Works Commissioner Bradford N. Clark.

Wagner said the academy symbolized the continuous progress that law enforcement had been making in the city and conveyed a bright promise for the future of both the city and its police force.

"With these new facilities," he added, "the Police Academy confronts the same complicated mission which everyday confronts the whole force – the enforcement of law and order. Law must be enforced. Order must be maintained. The police must be continually trained and schooled in this responsibility. Discipline, including self-discipline, must also be instilled. This is the mission of the police academy. It is a must in our city in this new day and age."[84]

The new academy arrived just in time. Back in 1961 Mayor Wagner was approached by Police Commissioner Michael Murphy, Patrick V. Murphy, Commanding Officer of the Police Academy, and Anna Kriss, Commissioner of Corrections, with the idea to create an entirely new CUNY police college, and the idea gained traction. While the municipal colleges were producing plenty of teachers, they were neglecting entry-level professional jobs like law enforcement, that were important to many students. The idea of the proposed police college was to fill this gap in the CUNY system. And despite some fear that the college would be controlled by the NYPD, the proposal for the new college was approved by the Board of Higher Education on June 15, 1964.[85]

Police Commissioner Michael Murphy was appointed acting president of the four-year CUNY police college. Murphy would work without salary in developing curriculum and faculty for the tuition free institution. Ten years earlier, as commander of the police academy, Murphy revamped the curriculum of that school, including the basic training for recruit police officers.

The plan was to house the police college in the new police academy at 235 East 20th Street. The college was to be open to policemen only, with the schedule geared to their off- duty hours.[86]

The College of Police Science (COPS) was established and admitted its first class in September 1965. Classes were originally conducted at the police academy for law enforcement officers only. Change began to take place in 1966 when the first civilian high school graduates were accepted into the College of Police Science, and in 1967 the college was renamed John Jay College of Criminal Justice.

1970 ushered in the most dramatic change with the era of open admissions at CUNY. There was now a guaranteed place at a CUNY college for every high school graduate who desired to attend college.

Open admissions profoundly affected all the CUNY campuses, but at John Jay it unleashed a hurricane of change that transformed the college. The size of the faculty doubled in 1971 and grew by another 25% in 1972. The number of undergraduates grew from 2,600 (one out of five of whom were civilians) to 6,700 in 1972 (over half were civilians), and finally to over 8,600 students in 1973. Suddenly, gone was the small institution devoted to police officers with classes in the police academy. What emerged was a medium sized, multipurposed college that eventually found its home on the West Side of Manhattan.

John Jay has since expanded its course offerings to provide undergraduate and graduate degree programs in a number of professional areas related to police and fire science, forensics, and cyber security. Today, John Jay is one of the nation's premier criminal justice and liberal arts institutions. The college brings together Pulitzer Prize-winning faculty and undergraduate/graduate students in diverse liberal arts disciplines to engage with issues of justice and diversity.[87]

When we look back on the history of the NYPD it turns out Commissioners Enright and Whalen were correct in their quest to mix police work with higher education. Those who scoffed at the concept of the Police College are likely spinning in their graves with the knowledge not only is there a 60-college credit requirement for employment with the NYPD, but that John Jay College of Criminal Justice grants NYPD officers 36 credits for completion of the Recruit

Academic Program at the New York City Police Department Academy.[88]

The College / Police Paradox:

In recent years there has been a debate in general society regarding the value and necessity of a college education, especially when weighed against the cost.

College education—also known as post-secondary education, tertiary education, or higher education—is a level of education that includes attending college, university, or vocational school. The rate of individuals pursuing higher education around the world has increased significantly over the last several decades—from around 100 million in 2000 to about 220 million today.

Now, college education is almost expected of most students in countries like the United States. But many people still ask the question, "Is a college education worth it?" It's an important question, as only about 40% of the global population has received some type of post-secondary or college education. So, when individuals decide to invest their time, energy, and money in a college education, what benefits are derived?

• Development and Growth - College education makes you grow and develop —both personally and intellectually. The main point of pursuing higher education is to further your learning and gain additional knowledge that you probably wouldn't have acquired otherwise. College is also likely to stretch and improve your critical thinking skills, which can help you better analyze, understand, and consider problems and situations. University-educated people build new knowledge for humankind's progress and growth.

• Preparation for Specialized Careers - Many careers—like becoming a doctor, a scientist, a teacher, and more—require a certain level of education and specific skills. If you are looking to pursue similar careers to these, then you almost always need to graduate from college—and often even obtain further education, like a Master's or Doctoral Degree. Going to college is the only way to become qualified for these types of jobs and prepare you for a career in a certain specialized field.

• Increased Earnings - The higher the qualification the higher the wages. While it's not true for each specific case, studies show that college graduates consistently out earn individuals without a degree. Over the course of a lifetime, a bachelor's degree is worth $2.8 million on average—75% more than that earned by a high school graduate.

• Economic Stability - Another one of the most important benefits of a college education is that it is more likely to result in economic stability for the individual and their family. Similar to increased earnings, this means that college graduates are more likely to be employed and financially stable than those without a degree—24% more likely. Education is also one of the most useful tools to prevent poverty, with the incidence of poverty being 3.5 times lower among college graduates.

Right now, you are likely asking yourself what did this commercial for college education have to do with the New York City Police Department? In 1993, the scandal at the 30th Precinct may have been the darkest moment in Police Department history. One-third of the patrol force was caught in its web, a grim testament to the transforming power of drugs and the havoc it wreaked in New York's most desperate neighborhoods.

Cops who were making $30,000 a year were confronted with car trunks full of hundreds of thousands of dollars, and for some, the temptation was too much. Thirteen police officers and a sergeant from the precinct were arrested for stealing hundreds of thousands of dollars in drugs and cash.

A common thread among those arrested was their low level of education: None held a college degree, and most had been cashiers or store clerks or were unemployed before they entered the Police Academy.[89]

In 1996 the NYPD increased the minimum education requirement for appointment from a high school diploma or equivalent to 60 college credits. Two years later, to ensure that candidates were presenting credits that were earned by responsible college level work, a 2.0 grade point index was required, the criteria that most colleges require to qualify for a degree.[90]

The college requirement was instituted to attract candidates who are better able to respond to difficult situations, especially in an increasingly complex city such as New York. A common thread among officers involved in inappropriate behavior was a low level of education and experience before entering the police academy. One observer noted that the common scenario in police recruitment and training involved selecting young adults right out of high school, rushing them through a five-month, police-operated training academy, giving them a gun, the authority to use deadly force and telling them to hit the streets. With the enormous amount of responsibility and public expectations placed on police officers, this college education requirement and the subsequent Police Academy training are still inadequate.

Good officers possess not only physical courage but also sound judgment, the ability to reason, knowledge of the law, and maturity. Adopting a college degree requirement, as opposed to requiring only 60 college credits without earning the degree, would allow the NYPD to hire well-educated, broad-minded officers who possess the maturity to deal effectively and in an even-handed manner with the public. Being a police officer means being part of a profession. Every major profession today educates its members through university-based education, except for the police. A completed college education would expose officers to humanities, social sciences, modern technologies, ethical issues, and the knowledge of the multidimensional aspects of crime and its impact on society. Additionally, a college degree requirement would help restore public confidence in the police by producing smarter and more mature police professional with proper training and who are less likely to succumb to the temptations of deviant behavior. With the many colleges in the City of New York providing a criminal justice education and degree, including the John Jay College of Criminal Justice of the City University of New York, city residents and the NYPD have ample opportunities to fulfill this requirement.[91]

Even though all evidence shows the correlation between education and a more effective police officer, the NYPD has actually taken steps backward since instituting the 60-college credit requirement. In 2000, faced with a dwindling number of applicants for the police academy, the NYPD relaxed its eligibility requirements to allow younger recruits to join the department and to admit more officers without two years of college.

Under the changes, the department accepted 21-year-old applicants. For the prior five years, the department set 22 as the minimum age, in the belief that officers younger than that were more likely to become disciplinary problems during their careers.

Police Commissioner Bernard Kerik said the department would waive a requirement that recruits have 60 college credits for two categories of applicants. The department already waived the requirement for those with two or more years of honorable military service. Now it waived the requirement for any of the city's 5,200 traffic enforcement and school safety agents with at least two years on the job. Kerik said the initiative was a creative way to enlarge the pool of qualified applicants and attract city residents to a career in the N.Y.P.D.[92]

Even today, more backwards steps are being considered as Mayor Eric Adams is contemplating scrapping the college credit requirement entirely.

Adams, himself a retired NYPD captain, entertained the idea after a closed-door meeting with Chicago Mayor Lori Lightfoot, whose administration recently scrapped a similar requirement for the Windy City's police department.

"I like what the mayor is doing in the recruitment. We're hearing all over the country that there is a requirement problem with police officers," Adams said during a joint press conference with Lightfoot at Chicago City Hall after their sit-down.

Under current protocols, NYPD officer applicants must have earned at least 60 credits from an accredited institution while maintaining a minimum 2.0 GPA. The Chicago Police Department dropped its 60-college credit requirement amid an ongoing struggle to attract new recruits. Under the new policy, Chicago Police Department applicants without college credits must have at least three years of professional experience in health care, education, social services or certain trade industries, or prior work in the security, correctional or law enforcement fields.

Adams, whose Chicago visit came after he traveled to Washington, D.C. to meet with Mayor Muriel Bowser, said it's critical for him to engage with his counterparts in other major U.S. cities.

"This is an entryway to learn from each other," he said.

Lightfoot, whose city, like New York, has seen a spike in gun violence during the pandemic, echoed Adams' sentiment. "I know we're going to be great partners," she said.

Which way will education in the New York City Police Department go? Only time will tell.

PHOTO GALLERY

Old Police Headquarters on Centre Street. The first official police academy opened in 1909 on the 4th floor.

Enright in 1918

Police Commissioner Richard Enright established a new
police academy in the City College Building on Lexington Ave.

New police academy was located inside the college building on
23rd Street and Lexington Avenue

Inspector John Noonan was placed in command of

The new police academy

Commissioner Enright appointed William "Big Bill" Edwards as Special Deputy Commissioner to oversee the academy.

An innovation at the new academy was the use of expert instructors, including celebrities, such as Harry Houdini and Benny Leonard

The picture shows Sergt. Julius Brilla (right) instructing Howard Peterson and Leonard Tobin (all of the New York City Police Department) in the gentle art of jiu-jitsu at the New York Police Academy, 23d st. and Lexington ave., Manhattan.

Most of the experts were non-celebrity members of the department

Capt. Charles B. Scully, director of life-saving of the American Red Cross, is shown demonstrating with Miss Helen Kourche how to render "downed" person to a swimming class from New York Police Academy.

Deputy Police Commissioner Edward Kelly is shown above presenting the honor graduates with the Bloomingdale Trophy, a service revolver.

Academy graduation ceremonies during the era were filled with pomp and pageantry.

Criminals will find it harder than ever to ply their nefarious trade in New York City today. This impressive array of policemen, 1447 in number, and the largest class to be graduated from the Police Academy, makes the city's force well equipped to cope with the criminal element. Mayor Walker is shown reviewing the rookie class with Inspector John J. Noonan.

By the time Grover Whalen was appointed police commissioner, the building housing the academy on 23rd Street had closed, forcing the academy to relocate to space inside the Grand Central Palace

Commissioner Whalen established the Police College across from
Police Headquarters on Broome Street and appointed Inspector
John O'Connell as Commanding Officer

POLICE COLLEGE DEAN

Deputy Inspector John J. O'Connell

MOTOR TRANSPORT SCHOOL

More than 1800 men in the motor transport school are registered for instruction. The course is very complete and experts furnished by manufacturers lecture. Principles and practice instruction run concurrently

The Police College provided training to recruits and veteran members of the department

"ROOKIES"

The disarming of criminals is one of the subjects taught and it is not elective either. The "rookies" become splendid athletes and are soon able to cope with brutes of the underworld

Policemen will be taught all about the traffic and lights on this floor.   It looks like the electric show but nothing is for sale.   The instruction is class work and demonstrations

The Police College was equipped with operating traffic signals that Officers would encounter on the street, and also provided training in how to properly file and perform administrative duties.

THE OFFICE FORCE

They may punch typewriters but they are all policemen, for police work is a man's job, except for the policewomen who have their own field looking after wayward girls, fortune tellers, and so forth.   They also receive special instruction in the Police College

A "dummy" loaded with weapons and dangerous instruments
was used as a training prop at the Police College. Policewomen also
received training at the Police College

Jujutsu Practice Teaches
Women Cops to Subdue 'Mashers'

Here are the old and the new of the Police Department. The large picture shows the cadets of the Police College swinging past the reviewing stand in yesterday's parade. The "Old Broadway Squad of 1890" is shown in the oval.

Whale of a Horseman Is Police College Dean

The dean of the Police College, probably, shouldn't be expected to be an expert horseman. He isn't, anyway.

While yesterday's police parade was forming, the dean was on horseback. A band started to play, and the horse started to prance. The dean, Deputy Chief Inspector John O'Connell, fell off the horse and landed in Broadway.

SENATE ADVANCES

The Police College used the annual Police Parade as an opportunity to put the recruits on display. In the 1930 parade, some members of the department wore 1890s style uniforms while the recruits sported a very collegiate style of dress

Policemen dressed in the uniform of the 1890s Broadway squad for the 1930 Police Parade. In the background are the Police College recruits in their collegiate outfits.

The recruits in their "parade uniform"
Newspapers spent a lot of time poking fun at the
Concept of a Police College

Edward Mulrooney succeeded Grover Whalen as police commissioner and oversaw the abandonment of the Police College

For twenty years after the Police College closed, the department
was forced to cope with two academy facilities that were woefully
inadequate. The first was on Poplar Street in Brooklyn, upstairs

from the 84th Precinct. Despite the cramped quarters, Commissioner
Mulrooney was determined to find space for the Police Museum

This novel instrument of crime in the hands of Patrolman Sullivan is a combination bat and pair of horseshoes. Right—Sergeant Joseph Evans holding a machine gun and a large carving knife, both implements seized by police in raids. These and many similar exhibits are being shown at the Police Academy, Poplar St. station.

The other inadequate academy was on Hubert Street on the
West Side of Manhattan. During most of the 1950s and
early 1960s recruits had to travel to Flushing Meadow in
Queens, and an armory in Brooklyn to complete physical training

The New York City Pavilion in Flushing Meadow and an armory where recruits received physical training

Police Academy Physical Training Session.

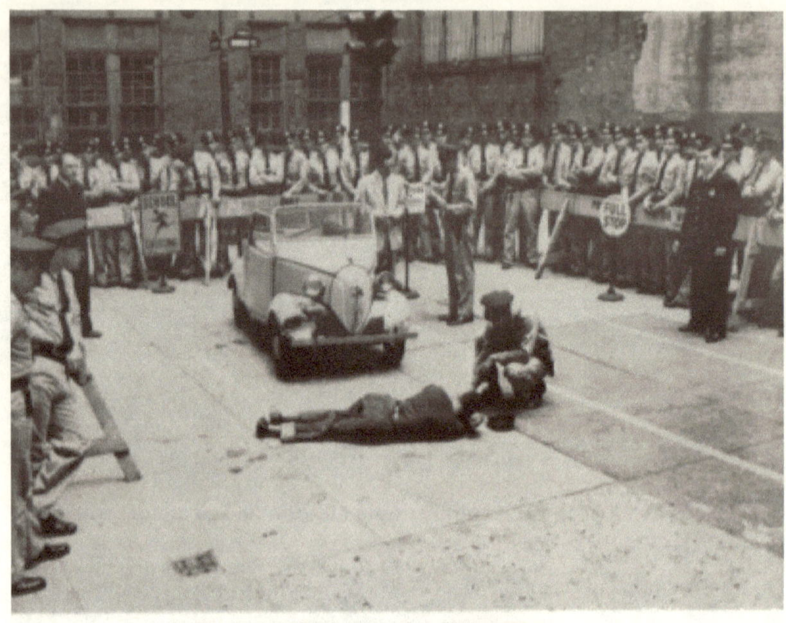

Recruits Receiving Practical Instruction at Police Academy
on Method of Handling an Accident Case

Instructing Recruits
at Police Academy
With Aid of the
Vu - Graph

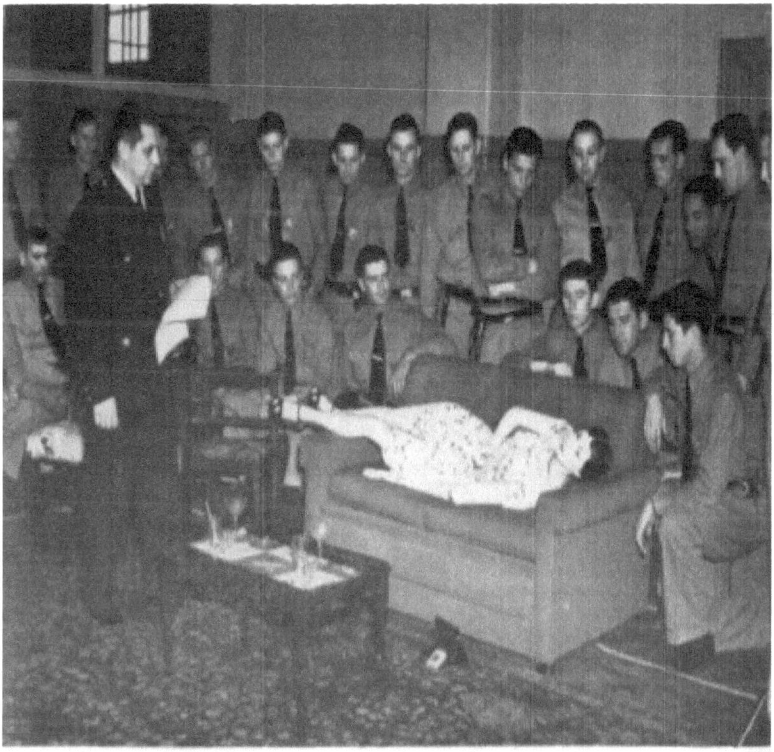

Recruits Receiving Instruction in Obtaining Evidence at Scene of "Homicide".

Training in shooting as well as in the handling and care of the revolver is a vital part of the instruction of recruits. Three hours a week during the recruit's training at the Police Academy are devoted to revolver instruction.

During the 1950s the department sought to attract college educated personnel, and finally located a site for a new police academy.

City to Break Ground for Police Academy on Monday

An artist's rendering of the new Police Academy, to be constructed on East Twentieth Street, between Second and Third Avenues. The building was designed by Kelly & Gruzen.

The police academy on 20th Street became the home of the College
of Police Science until the institution eventually departed the academy building
and became John Jay College of Criminal Justice

In 2014 the academy on 20th Street closed its doors and the new Police Academy is in College Point, Queens

The Broome Street Police College building and the Poplar Street academy site today

Bibliography

1. Justice For All: NYPD takes News 12 inside its police academy, July 2007, 2021
2. Bridglal, Brandon, WONDERLIST,10 Most Highly Trained Police Forces In The World
3. AIM OF POLICE COLLEGE IS MODERNIZED FORCE, The New York Times, 12/1/29, p150
4. HISTORY OF THE NEW YORK CITY POLICE DEPARTMENT, 1993, p4
5. AIM OF POLICE COLLEGE IS MODERNIZED FORCE, The new York Times, 12/1/29, p150
6. HISTORY OF THE NEW YORK CITY POLICE DEPARTMENT, 1993, p4
7. NEW YORK CITY POLICE DEPARTMENT ANNUAL REPORT, 1914-17
8. POLICE RECRUITS GRADUATE TONIGHT AT 69th ARMORY, The Times Union, 2/27/25, p23
9. FAVOR INSPECTOR NOONAN AS HEAD OF NEW ACADEMY, The Standard Union, 4/22/25, p5
10. ACADEMY FOR COPS OPENED BY ENRIGHT, The Brooklyn Daily Eagle, 4/24/25, p17
11. NEW YORK'S POLICE FORCE PERSONNEL CHANGES, Brooklyn Life and Activities of Long Island Society, 2/27/27, p2
12. WITH NOONAN AS COMMANDANT, The Standard Union, 4/25/25, p9
13. NEW YORK'S POLICE FORCE PERSONNEL CHANGES, Brooklyn Life and Activities of Long Island Society, 2/27/27, p2
14. POLICE ACADEMY INTENDED AS DEPARTMENT WEST POINT, The Standard Union, 5/2/25, p9
15. MacElhinny, John, LOOK OUT BELOW, The Brooklyn

Daily Eagle, 5/7/25, p21

16. ADD 275 NEW COPS TO CITY'S FORCE BY POLICE GRADUATION, The Brooklyn Daily Eagle, 6/6/1925, p3

17. BIG BILL EDWARDS TAKES OVER POLICE ACADEMY AND PROMISES TO AID COPS, The Brooklyn Daily Eagle, 6/18/25, p5

18. "BIG BILL" EDWARDS NAMED BY ENRIGHT AS POLICE DEPUTY, The Times Union, 6/11/25, p1

19. A PONDEROUS MATTER SETTLED, The Standard Union, 6/12/25, p10

20. POLICE TO HAVE COURSE IN ETHICS OF FOOTBALL, The New York Times, 6/21/25, p186

21. POLICE ADOPT FORD EFFICIENCY METHODS, The Times Union, 6/14/25, p3

22. HOUDINI NOW WARS ON MEDIUMS AS "PROF." AT POLICE ACADEMY, The Brooklyn Daily Eagle, 6/19/25, p4

23. HOUDINI IN DISGUISE BREAKS UP SÉANCE FOR STUDENTS: BENEFIT, The Tablet, 7/11/25, p1

24. HOUDINI ON SPOOK CATCHING, The Brooklyn Daily Eagle, 6/19/25, p6

25. BENNY LEONARD GIVES POLICEMEN LESSONS, The Times Union, 6/2/25, p13

26. POLICE ACADEMY PROGRAM ANNOUNCED BY EDWARDS, The Standard Union, 6/20/25, p7

27. EDWARDS QUITS JOB IN POLICE ACADEMY, The Times Union, 8/12/25, p20

28. TO MAKE ALL COPS AT HOME IN WATER, The Brooklyn Daily Eagle, 8/22/25, p18

29. UNTITLED, The Brooklyn Daily Eagle, 9/17/25, p3

30. ENRIGHT'S FINAL CLASS GRADUATES, The Times Union, 12/27/25, p10

31. GEORGE MCLAUGHLIN, BANKER, 80, DIES, New York Times,12/8/67, p42

32. WARREN WILL QUIT POLICE TODAY, New York Times, 12/13/28, p11

33. NEW ROOKIES ARE STUDYING HARD ON THE WAYS OF CROOKS, The Brooklyn Daily Eagle, 6/6/26, p10

34. POLICEMEN ARE MADE, NOT BORN, Albert A. Hoskins, Scientific American, April 1930

35. O'CONNELL TO HEAD NEW POLICE COLLEGE, The Times Union, 7/11/25, p2

36. WHALEN SEEKS NEW HEADQUARTERS, The New York times, 7/27/29, p1

37. NAME 50 TO TEACH AT POLICE COLLEGE, The New York Times, 8/6/29, p20

38. AWAIT OPENING OF NEW POLICE COLLEGE, The Times Union, 8/31/29, p5

39. 300 EMBRYO COPS WIN DIPLOMAS AT POLICE COLLEGE, The Brooklyn Daily Eagle, 7/2/29, p4

40. 259 ROOKIES, ONE JAPANESE, GRADUATED BY POLICE SCHOOL, The Standard Union, 7/2/29, p2

41. POLICE COLLEGE WINS NEW HONORS WITH LATEST GRADUATING CLASS, Times Union, 7/6/29, p5

42. NEW POLICE COLLEGE OPENING IS DELAYED, The Times Union, 9/7/29, p19

43. STUDYING THE POLICE SITUATION, Times Union, 9/7/29, p6

44. BRAINS THE NEW WATCHWORDOF POLICE AS BIG COLLEGE ENTERPRISE GETS A START, The Standard Union, 9/30/29, p16

45. WHALEN'S POLICE COLLEGE OPENS WITHOUT

CEREMONY, The Standard Union, 10/7/29, p3

46. AIM OF POLICE COLLEGE IS MODERNIZED FORCE, The new York Times, 12/1/29, p150

47. POLICE COLLEGE TRAINS MEN TO FIGHT NEW KIND OF CRIME, The Times Union, 10/16/29, p10

48. 59 TAKE COURSE AT POLICE COLLEGE, The Times Union, 11/2/29, p12

49. POLICEWOMEN UNDERGO HARD TRAINING, he Brooklyn Daily Eagle, 1/10/26, p10

50. WHALEN SEEKS $10,000 FOR POLICE PATHOLOGIST, The Brooklyn Daily Eagle, 11/5/29, p17

51. FIRST COLLEGE FOR POLICE ONCE CANDY PLANT, DEDICATED, The Times Union, 12/22/29, p86

52. POLICE COLLEGE GRADUATION HAS ACADEMIC TONE, The Brooklyn Daily eagle, 1/7/30, p6

53. POLICE COLLEGE ROBBED AS STUDENTS LEARN SCIENCE OF CATCHING PILFERERS, The Times Union, 1/8/30, p42

54. CITY LOANS POLICE TUTORS TO HOUSTON, The Standard union, 1/13/30, p17

55. STATE EDUCATORS DINED BY WHALEN, The Standard Union, 1/29/30, p5

56. DIPLOMAS FOR COPS, The Standard Union, 1/28/30, p2

57. CITY TO HAVE RAH RAH COPS IF NEW BAUMES BILL PASSES, The Times Union, 2/2/30, p119

58. UNTITLED, The Brooklyn Daily Eagle, 2/18/30, p20

59. CITY TO HAVE RAH RAH COPS IF NEW BAUMES BILL PASSES, The Times Union, 2/2/30, p119

60. UNTITLED, The Brooklyn Citizen, 1/26/30, p15

61. 527 GET DIPLOMAS AT POLICE COLLEGE, The Times Union, 4/1/30, p32

62. TIN HATS GRACE COPS IN BRILLIANT PARADE, The Brooklyn Daily Eagle, 4/27/30, p2

63. DUMMY GUNMAN SHOWS TRICKS OF GANGSTERS, The Brooklyn Daily Eagle, 5/9/30, p5

64. POLICE COLLEG INSTRUCTS IN AUTO HANDLING, The Brooklyn Daily Eagle, 5/11/30, p43

65. VIOLET DISPLACES GARDENIA AS MULROONEY TAKES POST, The Times Union, 5/21/30, p1

66. UNTITLED, The Times Union, 5/22/30, p22

67. CONFERS WITH WHALEN, The Standard Union, 5/21/30, p16

68. KONOWITZ JOINS POLICE COLLEGE, Times Union, 9/18/30, p12

69. STEEL CUTTING DRILL HELD, Times Union, 9/26/30, p8

70. POLICE ACADEMY, Times Union, 1/10/31, p5

71. NEW POLICE COURTESY SQUAD TO AID OUT-OF-TOWN VISITORS, The Standard Union, 7/1/31, p16

72. LEVY BALKS BUYING OF LOFT BUILDING, Times Union, 7/26/34, p4

73. PLUGGING ANOTHER LEAK, The Brooklyn Daily Eagle, 7/29/34, p24

74. POLICE COLLEGE IS DISMANTLED, Times Union, 7/27/34, p7

75. AYERS AND NOONAN QUIT POLICE SOON, Tines Union, 6/25/34, p1

76. BORO'S POLICE ACADEMY LEADS WORLD IN LATEST STUDIES TO STOP CRIME, Times Union, 11/25/34, p12

77. NEW ACADEMY BUILT OF POLICE OFFICIALS DREAMSTUFF, The New York Times, 9/1/64, p37

78. MAYOR REVEALS PLAN LINKING POLICE

ACADEMY WITH COLLEGE, Baruch College Archives, The Ticker, 9/21/54

79. UNTITLED, The Tablet, 6/16/56, p17

80. PD ACADEMY, CCNY, OFFER NEW SERIES, Greenpoint Weekly, 1/25/57, p5

81. CITY TO BREAK GROUND FOR POLICE ACADEMY ON MONDAY, The New York Times, 4/11/60, p14

82. POLICE ACADEMY WORK SET BACK BY STRIKES, The New York Times, 7/10/62, p23

83. NEW ACADEMY BUILT OF POLICE OFFICIALS DREAMSTUFF, The New York Times, 9/1/64, p37

84. OUR POLICE FORCE FASTES IN NATION SAYS MAYOR, Coney Island Times, 9/11/64, p4

85. PD ACADEMY, CCNY, OFFER NEW SERIES, Greenpoint Weekly, 1/25/57, p5

86. MURPHY TO HEAD POLICE COLLEGE, The New York Times, 8/31/64, p27

87. Picciano, Anthony, CUNY'S FIRST FIFTY YEARS: TRIUMPHS AND ORDEALS OF A PEOPLE"S UNIVERSITY, 2018

88. JOHN JAY COLLEGE UNDERGRADUATE BULLETIN, 2018

89. Jacobs, Andrew, The New York Times, Nov. 10, 1996, Section 13, Page 1

90. Berry, Mary Frances, Police Practices and Civil Rights in New York City, Report of the United States Commission on Civil Rights, August 2000, p164

91. Police Practices and Civil Rights in New York City, Chapter 2,Recruitment, Selection, and Training

92. Chivers, C.J., Police Relax Requirements For Recruits, The New York Times, Sept. 28, 2000, Section B, Page 1